LANDMARKS IN
WESTERN LITERATURE

LANDMARKS IN
WESTERN LITERATURE

BY

A. C. WARD

KENNIKAT PRESS
Port Washington, N. Y./London

LANDMARKS IN WESTERN LITERATURE

First published in 1932
Reissued in 1971 by Kennikat Press
Library of Congress Catalog Card No: 70-105845
ISBN 0-8046-1365-6

Manufactured by Taylor Publishing Company   Dallas, Texas

PREFACE

ALL map-making is a process of extreme but necessary simplification. This book is to be taken as a small-scale map of European and American literature, with certain areas treated as enlarged and more detailed insets. I am at a disadvantage in comparison with the ordnance map-maker, being unable to make use of any recognized symbols such as the cartographer employs to suggest the general character of the landscape. I must either crowd the page with a bewildering assemblage of names and references, or I must neglect the multitude of secondary writers whose work, as often as not, represents some important factor in a nation's genius. Without hesitation I have accepted the latter handicap, since I write neither for scholars nor informed critics, but for ordinary people who wish to learn their way about in world-literature. I assume that readers who have leisure and inclination to do so will fill my gaps by drawing upon more advanced studies.

There are those who hold that it is better not to read foreign literature at all than to read it in translation. If that were so, we English would have been impoverished of the English Bible and much else, while Shakespeare himself would have been at a disadvantage. In many instances, of course, translations fail to convey beauties of language and style and, sometimes, subtleties of meaning also. But human intercourse depends for the most part upon a community of ideas and the interchange of common impulses, rather than upon literary aesthetics or intellectual minutiae. Need English readers be debarred from the *Republic*, from Dante, *Don Quixote* and Tolstoy until Greek, Italian, Spanish and Russian are mastered in our schools? It may be necessary to ask this question from time to time until the rising wave of intellectual snobbery has become lost in the tide of liberal wisdom.

If my own acquaintance with foreign literature had done no more than extend my mental horizon and give me a sense of living in a larger world, I should be satisfied. Taking a broader view, I am confident that a general familiarity with the writings of other countries and other times would provide a steadier foundation for the League of Nations than the chancy deliberations of timid politicians. You cannot hate your neighbour so readily if you have enjoyed the books he writes.

Finally, a book of this present kind must be judged less by the information it imparts than by the appetite it stimulates.

In the Reading List beginning on page 183 I have enumerated the translations most easily available to the general reader, avoiding as far as possible expensive editions which appeal chiefly to scholars and bibliophiles. My thanks are due to Mrs. Constance Garnett for permission to quote from her translation of Dostoevsky's *The Brothers Karamazov*; to J. M. Dent & Sons Ltd. for passages from certain of their editions (see pages 14, 15, 46–50, 88); and to the Jowett Trustees and the Oxford University Press for an excerpt from Jowett's translation of Plato's *Republic*.

A. C. WARD

January 1932

CONTENTS

LANDMARKS IN
WESTERN LITERATURE

LANDMARKS IN WESTERN LITERATURE

CHAPTER I

GREECE

§ 1—*Ground Plan*

PASSING over the mass of oriental literature as outside the scope of this study, and beginning somewhat arbitrarily in Greece about 700 B.C., we find epic poetry already arrived at perfection in the *Iliad* and the *Odyssey* of Homer. What were the stages of development preceding that perfection remains a subject for inexhaustible conjecture, though it is now generally accepted that both Greek epic and Greek drama were culminating points, along diverging roads, of a development in which religious ritual celebrations had undergone gradual secularization and literary refinement. Accustomed as we now are to the conclusions of modern anthropologists and other scholars, it is fairly easy to follow the broad processes by which nature-myths and hymns to the gods emerged at length in the finished poetic art of a Homer or a Sophocles. The pity is that we can only speculate as to the details of the intermediate steps which led from the beginnings in religion to the ultimate achievements in art. Yet speculation is unlikely to lead us far astray if we start from the familiar phenomena of Night and Day, of Winter and Spring—seasons of darkness and decay supervening upon and preluding seasons of light and fruitfulness on which man depends for continued existence. What we now accept as the automatically governed procession of days and years was conceived by primitive man as being within the governance —the possibly capricious governance—of whatever gods he invented as engineers of his universe. If the succession of day to night, of spring and summer to winter was to be ensured, it is clear that the possibly capricious element in the make-up of the deities concerned had to be minimized to the last degree by whatever offices man could use to give satisfaction to his divine overseers.

When the Greeks had progressed so far in the union of ideas of religion with ideas of beauty as are represented in the figures of Apollo the sun-god, Dionysus the wine-god, and a hundred others, it is not surprising that their services before the gods—their ritual hymns—should also have reached an advanced stage of poetic and aesthetic accomplishment. The whole body of Greek mythology represents the illumination of an originally ominous mass of superstition by the light of emotional and intellectual fervour. To the artist it is second nature for men to appear to be like gods, uplifted as he is by an inspired consciousness of some more than human heritage ; and in the vision of men who have experienced this sense of godlikeness, the gods inevitably suffer some mitigation of the divine stature in which they appear to ordinary men. In a modern conventicle, a cultured hearer possibly finds it difficult to suppress impatience and some disgust as he listens to the diffuse and stammering prayers of fervent but unlettered worshippers. Yet the man who frames his prayers with a nice sense of shapely periods (as for example Robert Louis Stevenson did) will be moved less by a sense of his unworthiness before the deity than of his own ability as a maker of phrases presumably pleasing to the Maker of all. A rare unselfconsciousness is necessary in an artist, whether poet or painter, if he is to be altogether free from the sensation that, in their very different degrees, he and his god are both creators; and where this sensation is present, religious ideas cannot escape secular adulteration. Just as that secular adulteration took place in the medieval religious drama in England, so (though it is less plainly documented) it must have taken place in the development of Greek poetry and drama. The artist who feels himself on more or less familiar terms with the god, prepares the way for lesser deities and exalted humans such as Greek literature had profusely in its demi-gods and heroes. It can be seen, therefore, how religious invocations, when subjected to the artist's egotism and alchemy, may change in course of time into the celebration of men's heroic deeds: the human stature appears to be increased as the divine becomes less awesome—though it is only in the few periods of great creative power that characters in literature assume heroic proportions with an air of natural comfort.

We are unlikely to go far wrong if we regard the heroes in the *Iliad* and the *Odyssey* as representing an advanced (if not the final) stage of a rationalizing process whereby religious ritual, by disintegration, becomes transformed into the excellence of great poetry. Whether Homer was one or many has a chiefly academic interest, and concerning the date of the poems associated with that name it is sufficient here to ascribe them to about 900–800 B.C.

Even in the earliest times of myth and ritual, man was under no illusion as to the value of faith without works: he had to labour as well as to placate the gods. And so, when he acquired the habit of writing, epic poetry served not only for the narration of great deeds but also as a means for recording homely and practical information. In Greece, more or less contemporaneously with Homer, Hesiod (*c.* 850–800 B.C.) produced, besides the *Theogony* (Origin of the Gods), the *Works and Days*, which combines mythology and religious and moral commandments with hints upon everyday farm work, such as the selection of the most suitable material for plough-beams and waggon-building. He tells what wood is freest from worms and at what season it should be cut ; the best age for plough-oxen and plough-men, and what food the latter should be given : ' Let a man of forty follow the plough, his dinner a loaf of four quarters, eight pieces, who will mind his work and drive a straight furrow, no more gaping after his fellows, but having his heart in his work. Than he no younger man is better at sowing. For the mind of a younger man is fluttered after his age-fellows.' The *Iliad* and the *Odyssey* are works of art. No such claim can be made for Hesiod's poems : these are in part the exhortations of a teacher and in part a repository of practical knowledge and current superstition.

The progress from ritual to literary art can be followed more clearly in the dramatic than in the epic poets. The importance of vine-culture as a staple industry of the Greeks enlarged the importance of Dionysus the wine-god, making him a symbol of the earth's fertility as well as the divine embodiment of joy and ecstasy. The several festivals of Dionysus, therefore, were particularly significant to the Greeks and became the pivot of the year's ritual celebrations. This was specially true of the Great Dionysia, held in March each year. From the time when, at local festivals, the villagers and townsfolk chanted a dithyramb (an ecstatic and rhapsodic hymn) to Dionysus, we can trace the development of these choral songs through degrees of increasing complexity and elaboration to the point at which they issue in the splendid achievements of the tragic poets, Æschylus, Sophocles, and Euripides, a few of whose plays have alone survived from a vast number of works by many dramatists. The Dionysiac choral hymns were the starting-point for both tragedy and comedy, the more hilarious side of the festivals being departmentalized at length in the latter form. The simple chorus broke up first into dialogue between the leader and the rest ; then into dialogue between the leader and a single member of the chorus, with accompanying choral lyrics sung by the assembly. With additional minor developments, it was this stage that the Dionysiac celebrations had reached when Æschylus (525–456 B.C.) effected that further elaboration which made him the founder of tragedy as we know it. The single member of the chorus conducting a dialogue with the leader had been, in effect, an actor. Æschylus brought in a second actor, and made that part of the performance which was conducted by these two distinct from the choral portion. But it must be emphasized that now and always Greek tragedy retained much of its religious character; and the chorus remained, to the Greeks, the true centre of the whole affair. It is because we now find it virtually impossible to recapture the ritual significance and solemnity of Greek tragedy, and because we know too little of the management of the chorus, that we seek to assign to the chorus a specific function which satisfies our rational modern minds. We can speak with truth of the chorus as fulfilling (almost always) the part of 'ideal spectators', of detached observers; and we can with good reason find in the exquisite poetry of the choral lyrics a means of relief from the emotional tension created by the clash of tragic forces. But there is that something more at the heart of the choruses which eludes us, and makes our response to Greek tragedy vitally different from the original experience. Of the conditions under which the Greek plays were produced and of the modifications introduced by Sophocles (495–405 B.C.) and Euripides (480–406 B.C.) something will be said later.[1]

Tragedy is eternal and universal; comedy often local and occasional. Partly for this reason and partly also because our knowledge is less detailed, Greek comedy has received comparatively little attention. We know the names of a good many Greek comic dramatists, but apart from

---

[1] See § 3, pp. 17 ff.

Aristophanes' eleven plays (he wrote more than fifty) few works are extant. Aristophanes was an amusing, brilliant, and penetrative satirist of contemporary political and social organization, and he employed the usual bitter satirist's tongue against persons as well as institutions. Euripides is his most frequent butt, and it is typical of the manner in which current jokes miss fire in a later age that Aristophanes obviously extracted much amusement from repeated allusions to Euripides' mother as a greengrocer or herb-seller. But despite such esoteric touches, much of Aristophanes' fun can still be ' got across ' on the twentieth-century stage even to an uninstructed audience. Moreover, in such a play as *Lysistrata*, Aristophanes contrives to be more modern than ourselves, when he represents a feminine revolt against the war-mongering male with a vow of voluntary chastity as the chief weapon—the success of the campaign being imperilled because the women themselves find such self-denial too exacting.

Under Pericles in the middle of the fifth century B.C. Athens produced many of the chief glories of Greek literature, architecture, and sculpture. That century not only gave us the tragic and comic masterpieces in drama, but also saw Greek prose rise to greatness in the histories composed by Herodotus (*c.* 484–428 B.C.) and Thucydides (*c.* 471–400 B.C.). Somewhat later (431–354 B.C.) came the third great Greek historian, Xenophon. These three carried history from the time of the Persian, Cyrus (beginning 560 B.C.), down to 362 B.C., when Sparta and its allies were defeated at Mantinea in Arcadia by the Theban leader, Epaminondas. Each of the three writers had his own distinctive method as an historian, and all three achieved literary masterpieces. Herodotus was certainly not a scientific historian, but no one laments his deficiencies in that respect. Uniquely gifted as a narrator, he was inexhaustibly curious. His *History* sweeps along, taking within its current both fact and legend, and frequently deviating from a direct course in order to touch some social or geographical province which interested him. And the communication of this interest to readers through more than twenty centuries maintains the *History* of Herodotus among the freshest things in literature. Thucydides ranked accuracy above romance and is more academic (in the best sense) than Herodotus, though his accuracy is not of the modern documentary type. It is dramatic, rather, and consists largely in the reconstruction of the speeches delivered on critical occasions by historical personages. He secures both an appearance of detachment and the effect of intensity—sometimes tragic intensity. Xenophon is more directly personal. His *Anabasis* describes the incidents of the Greek expedition into Persia in 401 B.C., which he joined : the hopes and fears and dangers of the two years' march of the Ten Thousand are wonderfully and imperishably related. In the *Cyropædia*, dealing with the education of Cyrus the Persian, Xenophon combined history, philosophy, and fiction. He also wrote several discourses which entitle him to be considered as the originator of the prose essay.

We cannot get a proper view of Greek literature unless we appreciate that the spoken word had at that time an importance and attraction beyond what we ourselves attach to it, even in days when broadcasting should have revived the faculty of intelligent listening. Sounds, whether in speech or music, are to us little more than a background of noise, but to the Greeks the spoken word was almost the pivot of existence. Naturally, therefore, the art and craft of human speech were highly developed among them, and oratory reached such excellence as it has rarely equalled and never surpassed since. Demosthenes (384–322 B.C.), the most eminent Greek orator, was a practical politician and an able military strategist as well as an artist in prose. A devoted and enthusiastic Athenian patriot, he used oratory as a means of instilling his own exalted patriotism into the people of Athens. His speeches against Philip of Macedon, the invader of Greece, have added the word *philippic* (an utterance of invective) to our language; his persuasive power as a speaker was enormous, whether in the field of public leadership or in law cases; and the importance he assumed in enemy eyes is perhaps best illustrated by the fact that Demosthenes committed suicide by poison rather than risk capture when the Greeks at length went down before the Macedonians.

Just as the spoken word was an important weapon in statecraft and military affairs, so was it also the thinkers' primary channel for transmitting ideas. By Socrates' time the old Olympian gods were growing shadowy, and speculative inquiry into the nature of things had become persistent. Though Socrates is a vividly seen and heard figure to us still, no actual work of his survives. So far as we are concerned he is the creation of Plato, who became Socrates' pupil at the age of about twenty, and remained with him until the old man's execution some ten years later (399 B.C.). We judge that Socrates' whole life was devoted to a persistent quest of first principles and ultimate truth—the chief bugbear of most politicians, who are anxious that words and phrases shall be taken as current coin without inquiry into their precise significance. If Socrates had lived to-day in London he would have gone about the streets worrying young men and young women to tell him exactly what they mean by the glib use of such words as socialist, capitalist, Bolshevik, Fascist. Inasmuch as our modern democracy is in a large measure upheld by the unintelligent and abusive use of such catchwords (which save us from the dangerously destructive habit of thinking for ourselves), any influential inquirer—Socrates or another—would be assailed by the popular press as a corrupter of youth and an enemy of the people, and be quieted by the administration of whatever now corresponds to the Greek cup of hemlock. But after Socrates died from judicially commended poison, what was potent in his teaching survived vigorously in Plato's dialogues, directed as they are toward the Socratic goal of discovering what is the good life and how man may live it. To the pursuance of that inquiry by the poet-philosopher Plato we owe the sequence of discussions, crowned by the *Republic*, in which beauty and profundity are equally inexhaustible. Plato taught in the Academy on the outskirts of Athens, and had among his pupils the young Aristotle (384–322 B.C.), who was to rival him as the intellectual master of the western world for centuries to follow. If Aristotle had a more sheerly structural intellect than Plato he had practically nothing of Plato's poetic vision. Aristotle is above all a scientific philosopher; Plato a poet-philosopher: a difference which, as modern science is now beginning to indicate, may finally turn to the advantage of Plato, since great poets know from the first what scientists grope toward with patient industry and devoted labour. Ethics, Logic, Politics, Poetics, Natural History—all knowledge in fact—were scientifically analysed and systematized by Aristotle. He was intensely interested in what might be called the mechanism of knowledge, and this led to his formulation of the science of Logic in the aptly named *Organon*—meaning the ' tool ' which is the student's instrument for acquiring knowledge in a soundly systematic fashion. Poet as he was, Plato was less concerned than Aristotle with *means*, and it is this concentration upon means that makes Aristotle so much less attractive to the general reader, who is more interested in finished products than in processes. Yet, in general, Plato and Aristotle agreed that man is a *political* creature. Men must live together, and live together for the common good under such conditions as enable them to attain the right end of living— namely, happiness, which is ' an activity of soul in accordance with perfect virtue' (Aristotle's *Ethics*), a conclusion that necessitates (and is accorded) an inquiry into the nature of virtue. In Aristotle, as elsewhere in Greek philosophy, the conjoint ideas of goodness and happiness are inseparably associated with the idea of function. Thus, the good man is he who completely and without friction fulfils his function ; not solely his function as carpenter, or tanner, or what not, but his function *as man*. The determination of the nature of that function is, throughout, a leading factor in Aristotle's works, particularly in the *Ethics* and the *Politics*.

It is convenient to point out here that the unifying principle in all Greek art and thought is the insistence upon the necessity of harmony and balance—nothing too little, nothing too much—neither too much ' goodness ' nor too much ' badness '. Virtue, says Aristotle in the *Ethics*, ' is a kind of mean ; it aims at what is intermediate ', for ' virtue is concerned with passions and actions ' in which both excess and deficiency are forms of failure.

From the year in which Demosthenes and Aristotle died, Greek literature entered its final period of decline. Between 322 B.C. and the beginning of the Christian era there was little pure creative literature, except for the pastoral lyric poetry of Theocritus (*fl.* 283–263 B.C.) and his contemporaries, Bion and Moschus. Scientific literature had a distinguished addition in the *Elements* of Euclid (306–283 B.C.) ; and in history Polybius (*c.* 210–128 B.C.) carried on the good tradition. Much later, Plutarch (*c.* A.D. 40–*c.* 125), a Greek with Roman affiliations, wrote a series of nearly fifty ' parallel lives ' of eminent Greeks and Romans, a still fascinating collection which not only (through North's translation) assisted Shakespeare with his Roman plays, but also established biography as a literary form. The influence of Plutarch on English biographical writing can be traced in authors so far apart as Boswell and Lytton Strachey.

Echoes of the *Idylls* of Theocritus are frequently heard in

subsequent poetry—in the Latin and in our own.   There
is much elaborate craftsmanship in Theocritus, but, also, much
pleasing representation of simple country sights and sounds :

> Once thievish Love the honeyed hives would rob,
> When a bee stung him : soon he felt a throb
> Through all his finger-tips, and, wild with pain,
> Blew on his hands and stamped and jumped in vain.
> To Aphrodite then he told his woe :
> ' How can a thing so tiny hurt one so ? '
> She smiled and said, ' Why, thou'rt a tiny thing
> As is the bee : yet surely thou canst sting.'

This nineteenth idyll (translated, by Calverley, as *Love
Stealing Honey*) is a ' conceit ' that does not abate its charm
even when placed beside the more ' natural ' passages in
Theocritus : for example (from *Idyll* V) :

> Here falls a cold rill drop by drop, and green grass-blades uprear
> Their heads, and fallen leaves are thick, and locusts prattle here.

Yet notwithstanding the delightfulness of Theocritus, we
cannot read him without being aware of a certain lassitude
that accompanies culture in its second stage, when artifice
and deliberation have been called upon to cover a slackening
of the original fiery creative impulse.   Greek literature at
its best was an outcome of the fusion of art and experience.
But as we trace the passage of antique literature into the
penumbra of Græco-Roman civilization it becomes increasingly derivative ; its constitution is sometimes anaemic,
its countenance hectic ; the glow of the first robust vigour
has faded.

§ 2—*Homer*

Whether Homer was one or many is an unsettled question
which need not interfere with our enjoyment of the poems
that go under his name.   When we trouble to think about
the matter at all, it seems probable that the *Iliad* and the

Odyssey as they exist to-day are the work of an assembling and organizing genius who put together or perhaps only refined and polished a previous putting-together of lays that had had a long currency as the stock-in-trade of generations of minstrels. But, on the whole, this theory is less picturesque than the tradition that Homer himself was a wandering minstrel, an Asiatic Greek born (somewhere about 1000 B.C.) possibly in Smyrna, and that he became blind and poor in old age after a life given to the composition and recitation of these great epic poems. The only weakness of the tradition is its unlikeliness, for perfect works of art on the grand scale rarely spring full grown from the heads of travelling singers. Moreover, the varying levels of civilization and cultural achievement represented in the two poems indicate a longer period of gestation than one-man authorship could make possible. The only assured facts are the existence of the poems and the certainty that they provided the basis for Greek literature and learning. The Homeric poems are a great repository of myth upon which writers have never ceased to draw, and which provided the staple of subject-matter for all the great Athenian imaginative writers. In all probability they are a composite of history, fiction and religious legend, the several strands being so skilfully interwoven and finished with such consummate poetic artistry that they are now a unity showing no obvious joins.

The *Iliad* treats of the end of the Trojan war, after the campaign had run an indecisive course for nine years. In the beginning (before the poem opens) Eris, the goddess of Discord, had thrown into an assembly of the gods an apple which, marked ' for the fairest ', was claimed by Hera, Aphrodite and Athena.[1] Paris (son of Priam, king of Troy),

[1] As many English readers have grown accustomed to the Greek deities and heroes under their Latin names, it may be convenient to give here the alternative forms for those referred to in the text : Hera (Juno), Aphrodite (Venus), Athena (Minerva), Poseidon (Neptune), Ares (Mars), Zeus (Jupiter), Hephæstus (Vulcan), Odysseus (Ulysses).

appointed by the gods to give judgment, awarded the apple
to Aphrodite. Thereafter, Paris, visiting Sparta, carried off
Helen the wife of Menelaus and transported her to Troy.
Menelaus enlisted the help of other Greek tribal chieftains
to fit out an expedition against Troy for the recovery of
Helen. The Greek chieftains (or heroes) included Achilles,
Nestor, Ajax, Odysseus, and others, with Agamemnon
(brother of Menelaus) as leader, Hera, Athena and Poseidon
aiding them. The Trojans, with Priam as king, had Helen
and Paris, with the benevolent oversight of Aphrodite and
Ares. Zeus and Apollo held aloof. Opening with the
account of a quarrel between Achilles and Agamemnon (who
had carried off Chryseis, a priest's daughter, and brought
down a pestilence upon the Greek army), the *Iliad* throughout its length has *the wrath of Achilles* as its central and
unifying theme.

In approaching Homer and other Greek writers it is well
to keep always in mind their essential aims and ideals if we
are to regard certain literary characteristics aright as excellences and not weaknesses. Modern writers have accustomed
us to a type of literature which reflects the involutions and
complexity of the modern mind. The Greek mind was
simple and direct : not because it was incapable of subtlety,
but because it preferred plainness. So that whereas much
modern literature is marked by opulence and complexity,
Greek literature rejoices in the antitheses of such qualities.
The Greeks would have nothing to do with inessentials and
superfluities ; and we who are accustomed to the decoration
and elaboration of romantic art may feel that we are richer
than they. But the Greeks were so far right that they were
safeguarded against the accumulation of lumber. They
were artists, however, not ascetics ; they neither despised
nor rejected whatever properly subserved their ends. If
their ideal was *no excess*, it was, equally, *no inadequacy*. If
they cut away what was inessential, they as carefully

preserved all essentials. This is the true nature of classical
literature and art in its original manifestation. The disrepute which has sometimes in later generations attached
to the word ' classical ' was not always undeserved, since
modern classicists have inclined toward the false doctrine
that pruning is in itself a virtue. We may feel that there is
much to be said for the rigid economy of a Racine, but it is
doubtful whether the Greeks would have approved of such
work as his. They would probably have found it deficient,
debilitated, emaciated, ascetic. The Greeks favoured none
of those qualities, and we should insist upon the positives
in their work—adequacy, harmony and balance—more than
upon the negatives—economy, simplicity, clarity. Thus
Homer, though he is simple and clear, knew what means
were necessary to produce desired effects. He knew that
to say merely ' the great army gathered ' would be absurdly
inadequate to stir the blood and imagination of an audience.
Therefore he employed one of those many famous Homeric
similes which serve for that something more than description
which he desired :

Forward they marched, filling the air with the flash of bronze,
bright as the blaze of a forest fire, flaming upon a mountain-peak.
Out to the Scamander plain they streamed, like flock on flock of flutter-
ing cranes or long-necked swans in the meadows by the river-banks,
flying further and further, settling and rising again, calling to one
another so that the whole field rings with their cries. And the ground
echoed to the tramp of the marching feet and the sound of the horses'
hoofs, till they took their stand in the flowery plain, close set as the
leaves in spring.[1]

Homer, time and time again, wanted more than a visual
image ; he wanted an imaginative stimulus to start all the

[1] After comparison of the several ' standard ' verse and prose translations of Homer mentioned in the reading-list on page 183, I have quoted
from Marvin, Mayor and Stawell (*The Story of the Iliad*) which has
the advantage of a natural modern English idiom without ' period '
effects.

senses working. He found that stimulus in his wonderful
similes which are, as it were, draughts of poetic wine. Yet
it will be noted that these similes are free from false elaboration, artificiality, or straining for effect. All his picturing
is simple and natural and *within the common experience of
Greek listeners*. How otherwise could his effects have been
secured ? People are not stirred by hearing of things
beyond their comprehension ; and whatever a modern
literary poet may prefer, a wandering minstrel desired less
to show the poet's knowledge and cleverness than to fire
his audience to appreciative generosity. Homer is equally
able, too, in rendering human emotions in such a way as to
make them felt anew by whoever reads or hears his manner
of reporting them. If his ability in this direction were
confined to the valour of men or the love and courageous
endurance of women it would be less remarkable, even in so
fine a passage as the farewell of Hector and Andromache at
the end of Book VI in the *Iliad*. But Homer was fully
alive to the primary emotional significance of certain
secondary actions, and he never missed an opportunity.
Hector met his wife Andromache in the streets of Troy by
the Scian gate ; the nurse was with her carrying the child.
Toward the end of the farewell

Hector held out his arms to take his boy. But the child cried and
shrank back to his nurse's breast, frightened at all the armour and the
great nodding horse-hair crest. His father and mother laughed aloud,
and Hector lifted the glittering helmet from his head and laid it on
the ground, and then he took his darling son. . . .

The childish terror of the boy, the parents' laughter, and
the doffing of the helmet are pieces of exquisite by-play, and
their introduction at that point in the scene witnesses to
Homer's perfect artistry as well as to his subtle understanding of human nature. Homer's truthfulness, whether in
this faculty of detecting the essential importance of the
apparently unimportant or in more extensive matters,

cannot be overpraised. He is writing of heroes, of creatures who might be thought beyond average stature and unsusceptible to average weakness. But to Homer, heroes, too, are human. He sees them with admirable detachment, and declines to endow them with standardized heroic qualities or moral perfection. When Achilles kills Hector he behaves disgracefully toward his dead enemy. Paris, seeing Menelaus spring toward him, shrinks back like a poltroon and hides in the ranks. It has been remarked that Homer's attitude toward his heroes may be expressed in the saying of Anaxagoras, 'I was born to contemplate the works of Nature.' Men and heroes are to Homer the works of Nature (or of the gods), and he can be imagined as saying, 'It is not for me to make apology for the handiwork of the gods, nor to pass judgment upon them, nor to seek to improve upon what they have made. The gods made man; this is how man behaves.' If man is fearfully and wonderfully made, the poet's duty is to present man's fearfulness as well as his wonderfulness. Good and evil co-exist in man; therefore Achilles may well be at once generous and covetous, courageous and petulant, a hero toward the living and a savage toward the dead. Homer, again, was a Greek writing of a great war between Greeks and Trojans. Yet he does not appear as a Greek partisan, nor falsely glorify his nation, nor condone its faults. Homer's spirit in this was truly Greek, in setting honour above nationalism, and in giving no support, not even tacit support, to the doctrine of 'My country, right or wrong'.

Of Homer's skill as a literary craftsman very little can here be said. There is first and foremost, however, the very remarkable achievement of giving definite cohesion to a straggling group of stories by the unifying motive of the wrath of Achilles and by bringing the whole epic within the compass of a single year of the Trojan war. There is, further, the ability with which Homer distinguishes the many characters one from another without any of that exact particularization and mental analysis employed by modern writers. And, as a single example of his craftsman's skill and satisfaction in incidental passages, there is the renowned description of the new armour wrought for Achilles by Hephæstus, including the shield with its pictures of earth and heaven and ocean and of a multitude of things therein (the *Iliad*, Book XVIII). This is probably the finest piece of pure description anywhere in literature.

The *Iliad* is the national epic of ancient Greece. The *Odyssey* comes nearer to being a collection of fairy stories with a central hero. Thousands who know scarcely anything of the *Iliad* are closely familiar with the details of Odysseus' ten-years' wanderings after the fall of Troy before he reached his wife Penelope at their home in Ithaca. These stories are part of the legacy of every child from the cradle up, and it is almost as easy to imagine a sky without stars as a memory without Circe and the Cyclops and the lotus-eaters and the sirens among its stored riches.

§ 3—*The Tragic Dramatists*

In the vast open-air theatre of Dionysus on the hillside looking seaward below Athens it was possible to seat upwards of twenty thousand people. The multitudes that swarmed to the spring festival in the greatest days of Greek drama came to participate in a religious rite. In the centre of the almost circular arena—the orchestra, or dancing-place for the chorus—stood the altar to the god ; to the lowermost row of stone seats came the priests. From sunrise to sunset on three successive days, the audience listened to some of the greatest poetic creations ever born of the human mind and spirit. What have survived for us to value—

and these are possibly not the best—are enough to enable us to pass that judgment ; but incredibly many more of the plays have perished. It is overwhelming to think of what the modern reader's riches would amount to if we had those hundreds of Greek tragedies, instead of the score or two that actually remain. From what we have and from what we knew from other sources, it is possible to build up a fragmentary picture of the Great Dionysia in its yearly progress. The dramatists, having secured the patronage of a leading citizen who would bear the expense of a chorus, each entered a tetralogy [1] of plays in competition with those of other poets. Three of each group of plays were tragedies proper, the fourth was somewhat lighter in texture—a satyr play—of which Euripides' *Cyclops* and (possibly) *Alcestis* are examples. There were no women actors, and the conventions of the drama were such that movement (except in the choric dances) was almost eliminated, and there was no action in the modern sense : everything of a violent nature was reported by a character—usually a messenger, or a shepherd, or a soldier —who had witnessed the particular deeds off-stage. [2] A fixed stage-setting—usually the portico of a large house or palace or temple—allowed no variation of scenic effects, [3] and the use of painted metal masks (which probably served also as megaphones to amplify the actors' voices) precluded facial gesture. Buskins (padded boots) were used to increase the stature of the heroes and thus to give them

[1] Gilbert Murray, however, suggests that this was peculiar to Æschylus (see *Euripides and His Age*, Ch. III, p. 67).

[2] See Talthybius' account of the death of Astyanax in the *Trojan Women*; the messenger's story of the poisoned robe in *Medea*; the watchman's charge against Antigone of burying her brother's body in defiance of the king's edict, etc.

[3] This is true in general, though the use of a revolvable device permitted some modified suggestion of a change of place, and there were other mechanical devices, especially that for transporting divinities.

' tragic height '. It is only necessary to add that all the plots used by the dramatists were old ones entirely familiar to the audience, in order to point the conclusion that the element of surprise was non-existent in the Greek theatre, and the element of spectacle almost equally so. What remained ? There remained, on the secular side, the interest of the poet's individual treatment of a familiar theme (the difference, that is, for example, between Sophocles' *Electra* and Euripides' *Electra*, though these were not of course produced upon the same occasion) ; also the pleasure of hearing spoken poetry—and there is no greater joy possible to man, though we have now lost the habit. On the ritual side, there was the lingering sense of participating at a solemn celebration. The audience did not on that account suppress its more exuberant instincts, nor fail to record its frank opinion of the poets' worth ; but even when the original specifically religious intention had become muted, there was still the never-forgotten underlying idea of Greek tragedy, which gave it the nature of a spiritual and moral inoculation—using that word in the modern medical sense. We inoculate people with a small dose of a particular disease in order to increase their power to resist that disease and therefore to secure immunity from its natural onset in a dangerous form. The Greeks watched tragedies in which pitiful and terrifying things were represented as happening to others. They themselves imbibed some part of that pity and terror and were thereby strengthened to endure such trials as might come to them personally.[1]

Æschylus, the oldest Greek tragic dramatist whose plays have come down to us, marks a particularly interesting

[1] This is a simplified statement of Aristotle's famous theory of *katharsis* which he set down in the *Poetics*. Scholars have spent many generations discussing what he actually meant. My inoculation analogy seems at least plausible ; it conveys what I myself experience when watching a tragedy ; and I hope it is reasonably accurate.

stage in human intellectual and spiritual development. His work has a bare monumental greatness, a rugged mountainous aspect, when considered beside that of Sophocles and Euripides. Æschylus may be likened to a giant endeavouring to bring order out of chaos : his trilogy, the *Oresteia* (*Agamemnon*, *Choëphoroe*, and *Eumenides*), represents the transition from the savage age of revenge and wild justice to the reign of moral law. In Sophocles, a further stage has been reached. Moral order has been imposed upon the world, but it has set up conflicting loyalties. The idea of duty is a part of the moral order ; but how should we act when there is a conflict of opposing duties ? What is Antigone to do ? Her duty of obedience to the gods necessitates the performance of the prescribed burial rites over her dead brother Polynices. Her duty of obedience to the king, Creon, demands her subservience to his command that the rebel remain unburied. Justice demands that Antigone shall die because she violates one moral duty in performing what she considers a higher. Creon suffers for his brutality and injustice, but the matter is between himself and the gods ; whereas for Antigone, the subject, the matter is between herself and the king. 'The gods are just' and need no human hand to ensure or hasten their justice. Morally, *Antigone* may not satisfy twentieth-century standards : our sympathies are entirely with Antigone and against Creon. Some one has said that she was an early Joan of Arc—an entirely apposite remark. But Sophocles' problem was the same as that by which the Inquisition was faced : Let the Antigones and Joans loose in the world to go unchecked and what becomes of the moral (or the religious) order ? Antigone and anarchy ; Joan and apostasy ; the right of private judgment ; un-limited individualism ; and confusion all round. Given power, both Antigone and Joan must in the end come back very near to the position from which they sought to drive Creon and the Holy Fathers. In relation to *Antigone* (just as in the case of Bernard Shaw's *Saint Joan*) the issue is complicated for us by the creative ability of the dramatist. The beauty wherewith Sophocles has illumined Antigone's character inclines us to the feeling that she can do no wrong, and, independent of the moral dilemma, *Antigone* is immortal on her account. But we can at least imagine within a little what emotional and sympathetic significance this tragedy must have had for a Greek audience to whom the dilemma was a thousand times more actual than to us.

In contradistinction to Æschylus and Sophocles, Euripides was almost purely a humanist and a sceptic questioning rule and authority as such. Hatred of injustice and oppression was his ruling passion, and he castigated it wherever he found it. The *Trojan Women* is a contemporary political pamphlet, as well as a tragic masterpiece depending for permanent interest upon nothing but its intrinsic greatness. Yet in its own day and place, Euripides' obvious allusion to the Greeks' unjust and barbarous dealing with the people of Melos [1] during the Peloponnesian war must have come as a thunderclap to complacent nationalists. The analogy drawn inferentially by Euripides between the captured women of Troy and the ravaged islanders on Melos, informed as it is with the poet's intense passion, can be appreciated better if it is read side by side with Thucydides' account of the Melos affair. The historian relates the course of events with as little emotion as if he were describing the proceedings at a company shareholders' meeting. [2] His brief record of the actual tragedy forms scarcely more than an inconsiderable footnote to the detailed account of the preliminary negotiations and arguments : of human feeling and pity there is barely a trace.

[1] See Gilbert Murray's *Euripides and his Age*, etc.
[2] See *The Peloponnesian War*, Book V, Ch. XVII.

Over against this, there are the unforgettable lamentations of Euripides' Andromache over her own fate—

> Forth to the Greek I go,
>   Driven as a beast is driven—

and over that of her child, Astyanax, dashed down from the city walls by the Greeks lest he should grow to manhood and be as great a menace to the conquerors as his father Hector had been.   Euripides' sympathies are equally engaged in *Medea* on behalf of the woman who, made frantic by Jason's conduct, burns out one agony with the greater one of murder; while, in *Alcestis,* his tenderness is delicately shown in the mother's last words to her children.   *Alcestis* is unique in Greek drama because it is a tragicomedy, not a tragedy proper.   Taken apart from whatever ritual significance the character of Heracles may have, *Alcestis* might be described as the portrait of an egoist. Admetus is as confirmed an egoist as Meredith's Sir Willoughby Patterne, and there is hardly a more satisfying moment in literature than when his old father, Phêres, abused by Admetus because he had refused to die in his stead, makes a suitably robust reply.

Euripides' 'modernness' draws us closer to him than to either Sophocles or Æschylus, yet in a positive sense Æschylus' genius out-tops the others'.   His is a greatness that stretches above the human range, austere and remote, demanding veneration but not engaging love.   His *Oresteia* is the only surviving trilogy of Greek plays, and it is in more than the usual sense a landmark.   It is the Everest among tragedies, lofty, massive and majestic.   The vastness of Æschylus' genius enables him to get divinity as well as humanity within the compass of his intellect.   He sits in judgment upon gods, as well as upon half-gods and heroes and humans.   Euripides criticizes the gods and their actions ; he thinks, often, that they are evil ; but Euripides is rather like a courageous but homely mouse looking contemptuously at a king. Æschylus, however, is no rationalistic critic of the gods. Still less is he their enemy. He believes that the world needs supernatural controllers, but he wishes those controllers to be perfect and beyond reproach. The *Oresteia* may be regarded as the embodiment of the Old Law and the New Law among the Greeks. The first two plays, *Agamemnon* and the *Libation Bearers* (*Choëphoroe*), exemplify the old law of vengeance, ' an eye for an eye '. Æschylus seems to ask, ' What can this lead to but everlasting blood-feuds ? Are vengeance and retribution the last words of Zeus ? What is to be the end of this matter of the House of Atreus, with its bloody tale of woe and disaster hanging around Agamemnon and Clytemnestra and their offspring, Orestes and Electra ? ' Must not the blood-feud give place to a system of lawful procedure in which ' justifiable ' crime can find purification and pardon ? Æschylus appears to feel that even the gods must learn and receive more and more light, more and more wisdom, through a progressive revelation. So, in the *Eumenides*, Æschylus puts forward what might be called the New Testament of pagan Greece, creating a new dispensation in which is conceived the possibility of atonement for sin, with wise human counsellors and mediators between gods and ordinary men. The Furies are transformed into kindly Earth-spirits (the Eumenides) and the whole long riot of bloodshed is brought to an end with Orestes purified and pardoned, Athens established as the supreme city wisely guided by the Areopagus (Great Council) meeting on Mars Hill : that is, Righteousness, Justice and Peace are established on the stronghold of the God of War. In the *Agamemnon* and the *Libation Bearers* we feel as though the entire universe of gods and men is agonizing. The vast opening scene is dark, and the stabbing fires of beacons lit from hill to hill to announce the fall of Troy are like

spirts of blood upon the sky. Vengeance and horror and
the taint of blood hang across the world, until at length (at
the end of the *Libation Bearers*) Orestes flies almost in
madness, pursued by the Furies clamouring for his destruction. But in the closing play, madness is itself exhausted ;
the universe passes from its wild delirium, and the breath
of sanity comes to bring healing to tortured spirits. The
Furies instead of being allowed to fall upon Orestes and
tear him to pieces are compelled to prosecute him lawfully.
Apollo defends Orestes, the Great Council of Athens
serves as the jury, Athena is the judge—and her casting
vote sets Orestes free. The Furies, being converted,
become the guardian spirits of Athens, and the whole course
of events is resolved in an atmosphere of atonement and
reconciliation. If the Greeks believed that a principal
function of tragedy was to purify the human spirit, the
process of vicarious purification can rarely have been more
powerfully effected than by the *Oresteia*, which was performed in 458 B.C., two years before Æschylus died.

§ 4—*Herodotus*

Looking back at ancient Greece, we see no such divorce
between literature and life as often appears to exist to-day.
Poets were also soldiers and citizens, as citizens might be
poets and soldiers, and soldiers poets and citizens. So
Herodotus was not only a traveller and historian but also
a political leader and a literary artist. History was not
then for schools and scholars, but for the people ; and it
would therefore be in harmony with the common interest
that Herodotus should recite parts of his *History* at the
Olympic games, as he is reported to have done. This at
least ensured that history would have a living force and
dramatic intensity, and it is impossible to imagine a better

discipline for present-day historians than that they should be compelled to keep the waiting Cup Final crowd at Wembley Stadium breathlessly entertained with passages from their latest works. In historical writing accuracy and dullness are not enough, for the life which history sets itself to record is seldom accurate and never dull.

The *History* of Herodotus was designed to do more than teach the facts of national development. Throughout its length there is a thread of tragic warning in relation to the penalties that fall upon those who violate in their lives the principle of *No excess*. The *History* deals chiefly with the invasion of Greece by the Persians and with the ensuing war which lasted until 478 B.C. when the Persian domination was thrown off. Thus, in the end, the greatness of Persia was brought low by the littleness of Greece. Persia had become excessively powerful, excessively pros·perous, excessively wealthy. Overmuch wealth and prosperity and power led to insolence and blindness, and then ruin came. For Herodotus and the Greeks this was the tragic spectacle—the living parallel of such tragedies as Æschylus' *Prometheus Unbound,* where Zeus in the cruel arrogance of power tortures Prometheus and for a time seems to triumph over him. But the cruelty of Zeus, his lust of power, his insolent greatness, bring about his own downfall and make possible the triumph of the apparently puny humans whom Prometheus championed. But if the ultimate overthrow of the Persian Goliath by the Athenian David was a warning of the disaster that waits upon proud and arrogant strength, to Herodotus and other philosophically-minded Greeks the victory over Persia was also a warning to Athens. To the victor, victory should not be a cause of jubilation only. Through the humiliation of defeat, once-arrogant men and nations may learn wisdom and a proper humility ; while, through the intoxication of victory, conquerors may be lured to overweening pride and come thereby to doom. Greek thinkers who sought to know life in its fullness from first to last, were aware of the pitfalls that await men and nations upon whom the gods seem to shower all their gifts ; they were aware of the dark shadow cast by the bright sun. Even at the height of their national greatness the wise ones among the Greeks were a severely self-disciplined people 'who walked softly all their days, in the fear of the Most High and in the shadow of tragedy'.

Those who like to fix the parentage of literary forms have named Homer as the father of epic poetry, Æschylus the father of tragedy, and Herodotus the father of history. There were historians of a sort before him—Herodotus names one, Hecataeus—but of their works no more than fragments exist. Herodotus had an intimate and deep knowledge of Homer's poems and of other writers ; he was a tireless traveller who observed and studied closely. The material for his *History* was drawn from three main sources : (a) his own observations of peoples and their customs ; (b) what he was told by others—priests, etc. ; (c) his reading of earlier historians. If the writing of history is an art and not merely the compilation of records, then Herodotus is undoubtedly the first true historian. He had a developed sense of form which caused him to work upon his first draft as a sculptor works upon the stone, seeking a perfection of outline and mass. Of the nine books which comprise the *History* the last three are thought to have been written first : these contain the account of the Persian invasion. Afterwards he seems to have desired to link up the Græco-Persian war with the history of contiguous lands, and so proceeded to write the six introductory books, which are as near to being a universal history as could possibly be produced at that time. But, when all is said, the animation and freshness we still find in Herodotus' work come from those features which do not belong to plain history. If Herodotus were judged as an historian and nothing but an

historian, he might rank as high as Thucydides and Xenophon but not higher. His pre-eminence is due to the fact
that he was a great creative and imaginative artist, and
that the artist in him overrode the scholar. 'Whenever
he speaks from his own observations,' says Dr. William
Smith, 'he is a model of truth and accuracy; and the
more the countries which he describes have been explored
by modern travellers, the more firmly has his authority
been established.' But where he relied upon hearsay
Herodotus was often deceived. It has been pointed out,
for example, that the numbers he gives for the Persian army
'are incredible', over two million fighting men, plus half
a million to man the fleet, plus a great multitude of servants
and supply men—making a total of some five million;
whereas it is calculated that the Persians had probably
under half a million in all. Then, again, Herodotus'
undeveloped critical sense (or, we may prefer to think, his
glorious imaginative sense) led him to incorporate a wealth
of legends and strange stories—and it is this predilection
that makes his *History* the delicious book it is. Though
many among his travellers' tales have more than a touch of
the marvellous, they nearly all rest on this side of impossi-
bility; there is usually a substratum of credibility which,
by accretion, has grown to a wonder. He relates (Book III)
how Cambyses sent envoys to the Ethiopian king, from whom
they learn that most of the king's subjects live to be a
hundred and twenty and upwards.

When they showed wonder at the number of the years, the king led
them to a fountain, wherein, when they had washed, they found their
flesh all glossy and sleek, as if they had bathed in oil—and a scent came
from the spring like that of violets. The water was so weak, they
said, that nothing would float in it, neither wood nor any lighter
substance, but all went to the bottom. If the account of the fountain
be true, it would be their constant use of the water from it which
makes them so long-lived.[1]

[1] Rawlinson's translation.

We may think that fountain of youth unlikely, and yet any mineral spring, by the aid of folk-lore, might gain some such magical reputation.

The excellences of Herodotus are many, and his *History* is one of the most readable books in the world, largely because of his eye for picturesque detail which, on examination, is not always as irrelevant as it might appear. Characterizing the Persians, he writes (Book I) :

It is their general practice to deliberate upon affairs of weight when they are drunk; and then on the morrow, when they are sober, the decision to which they came the night before is put before them by the master of the house in which it was made; and if it is then approved of, they act on it; if not, they set it aside. Sometimes, however, they are sober at their first deliberation, but in this case they always reconsider the matter when they are under the influence of wine.

During the war between Ægina and Athens, a catastrophe befell an Athenian expedition and only one man escaped (Book V) :

When he came back to Athens, bringing word of the calamity, the wives of those who had been sent out on the expedition took it sorely to heart, that he alone should have survived the slaughter of all the rest ;—they therefore crowded round the man, and struck him with the brooches by which their dresses were fastened—each, as she struck, asking him where he had left her husband. And the man died in this way.

The women, as Herodotus proceeds to tell, did not go unpunished—though their punishment was more quaint than severe.

Illustrations might fitly be given of Herodotus' pathos [1] and of his humour,[2] yet it will be more proper to show that in addition to those qualities which give charm to the *History* and provide entertainment for us, there is also a

---

[1] See, for example, his account of the trials of the Egyptian king Psammenitus (Book III).

[2] E.g., Alcmæon's visit to Crœsus (Book VI).

majestic element. To the ambassador of Mardonius the
Persian general, who had been sent to press upon them the
hopelessness and peril of continuing the war, the Athenians
made reply (Book VIII) :

We know, as well as thou dost, that the power of the Mede is many
times greater than our own ; we do not need to have *that* cast in our
teeth. Nevertheless we cling so to freedom that we shall offer what
resistance we may. Seek not to persuade us into making terms with
the barbarian—say what thou wilt, thou wilt never gain our assent.
Return rather at once, and tell Mardonius that our answer to him is
this : ' So long as the sun keeps his present course, we will never join
alliance with Xerxes. Nay, we shall oppose him unceasingly, trusting
in the aid of those gods and heroes whom he has lightly esteemed,
whose house and whose images he has burnt with fire.' And come
not thou again to us with words like these ; nor, thinking to do us a
service, persuade us to unholy actions. Thou art the friend and guest
of our nation—we would not that thou shouldst receive hurt at our
hands.

That is drama as well as history, and it may serve as a single
indication of the strength constant in Herodotus' pages,
even when his mood is less controlled by the spirit of high
seriousness he uniformly displays when he writes concerning the actions and destiny of Athens.

§ 5—*Plato : The Republic*

Poets, dramatists, and historians will seem to belong to a
different order from common humanity so long as the plain
man persists in taking a romantic view of poets and dramatists and an academic view of historians. The philosopher,
however—hesitant though the plain man may be to believe
it—is very like the ordinary run of humanity, in regard
both to the subject-matter of his speculations and his
method of inquiry. Moderns have been heard to speak of
' that weary Plato ', and would no doubt go on to denounce

' those weary Platonic dialogues '.   But neither Plato nor
his dialogues are or ever were weary.   Plato was an energetic,
enthusiastic, inquiring person who gathered round about
him a company of the bright young people of Athens.   He
is not weary or dull; and if he is sometimes incompre-
hensible, incomprehensibility is as enticing as the mountain-
peak which is a little higher than the one just climbed.   A
Platonic dialogue can only preserve its strangeness for us
so long as we continue to think of it as something fixed in a
book.   If we remove it from the printed page and, as it
were, stage it imaginatively in our minds, a Platonic dialogue
becomes very much like a discussion scene from a play by
Bernard Shaw.   It is a company of people sitting round and
talking together for the same purpose as Bernard Shaw
makes his characters discuss—in the confident hope that
they may see truth dawn together.   No reasonable being
thinks it necessary to apologize for undertaking physical
gymnastics.   Philosophy is a mental gymnastic which gives
tone to the mind and braces the intellectual muscles, provided that we use philosophy properly and do not, by
losing ourselves in a swirl of words, get out of touch with
actuality.   Philosophy is an exemplary servant; it may
become a tyrannous master.

Before approaching the *Republic* as a document bearing
upon problems of human government and Statecraft, it will
be interesting to consider one of Plato's most famous con-
ceptions, in its character as a mental gymnastic : his *Theory
of Ideas*.   Plato took the view that a properly-ordered State
must be governed, not by that casual assemblage of amateur
legislators which constitutes a democracy, but by a specially selected and carefully trained body of people—he calls
them philosopher-kings.   Only a philosopher, he held, is
fit to rule.   What then is a philosopher ?   A philosopher,
according to Plato, is one who *knows reality* and can attach
himself and others to reality.   In the endeavour to answer

the obvious further question, *What is reality ?* the Theory
of Ideas begins. From the outset it is necessary to distinguish between the Platonic and the modern colloquial use
of the word *ideas*. We ourselves may say that a man has
'strange ideas', when we actually mean that he holds
strange opinions. Plato meant the opposite of this, for
Ideas were to him the antithesis of opinions. One person
may be of opinion that a particular piece of sculpture is
ugly ; another may think it beautiful. We should say that
either one or other is ' wrong '. Plato would have said our
piece of sculpture exists only in the world of opinion, of
sense, or appearance—not in that world of Ideas which
contains the only true realities. The piece of sculpture is
something which ' participates in ', or has in part the
nature of, Beauty (or of Ugliness). It is only a shadow-
shape of which the ultimate reality is Beauty (or Ugliness).
Beauty is real ; Ugliness is real ; Whiteness and Greenness
are real. But a beautiful flower, an ugly building, a white
collar, a green leaf are not real in Plato's philosophical
meaning ; they are shadows seen by us in our world, which
is the world of sense or appearance, not of reality. Plato's
Reality is in a world beyond ours where exist those Ideas,
or Forms, or Universals (or, as the Christian might say, the
heavenly patterns) which are alone *real*. We can agree
that a white collar is not the reality Whiteness ; as we can
agree that the symbol we use to represent a point . is not
the *Idea point*, which has position but no magnitude. Our
symbol . obviously has magnitude, to whatsoever degree of
fineness we reduce it ; but the Idea is a concept existing
only in that state which is Plato's unseen world of Reality.
This is the myth Plato uses :

Behold ! human beings living in an underground den, which has a
mouth open towards the light and reaching all along the den ; here
they have been from their childhood, and have their legs and necks
chained so that they cannot move, and can only see before them,

being prevented by the chains from turning round their heads. Above and behind them a fire is blazing at a distance, and between the fire and the prisoners there is a raised way ; and you will see, if you look, a low wall built along the way, like the screen which marionette players have in front of them, over which they show the puppets.

I see.

And do you see, I said, men passing along the wall carrying all sorts of vessels, and statues and figures of animals made of wood and stone and various materials, which appear over the wall ? Some of them are talking, others silent.

You have shown me a strange image, and they are strange prisoners.

Like ourselves, I replied ; and they see only their own shadows, or the shadows of one another, which the fire throws on the opposite wall of the cave ?

True, he said ; how could they see anything but the shadows if they were never allowed to move their heads ?

And of the objects which are being carried in like manner they would see only the shadows ?

Yes, he said.

And if they were able to converse with one another, would they not suppose that they were naming what was actually before them ?

Very true.

And suppose further that the prison had an echo which came from the other side, would they not be sure to fancy when one of the passers-by spoke that the voice which they heard came from the passing shadow ?

No question, he replied.

To them, I said, the truth would be literally nothing but the shadows of the images.[1]

Aristotle, Plato's pupil, disputed the whole theory, insisting that it made the elementary error of postulating an objective being for what are nothing more than mental concepts which do not exist as realities in some supranatural 'real' world, but only as notions in our minds. There is much more than this to be said for Plato, however, if we consider his theory in relation to matters that are at once more abstract and yet at the same time closely practical. Instead of dwelling upon the very amusing problem

---

[1] Jowett's translation

of whether white mice are really white or really mice or
really anything at all other than symbols or shadows of
another world in which whiteness and mousiness are *real*,
let us put aside mental gymnastic and turn to the fundamental matter of inquiry in the *Republic* : How to organize
the perfect social and political State. What is men's aim
when they set out to establish a perfect community or
Society ? The aim is goodness. And the pre-essential to
goodness in Society is a society composed of good men.
A man is good when he is just and holy. What do we
mean by justice and holiness, and how may a man acquire
these virtues ? Or what, rather, causes a man to be unjust
and unholy ?—Lack of knowledge ; that is, ignorance. He
is wanting in true knowledge, which would convince him
that peace of mind (the greatest blessing that man can
possess) is the product of justice and holiness. If men are
content to believe that the law of their country is justice
and its religion holiness, they are in grievous error. The
law of a country may partake of the nature of justice, but
it is not in itself Justice. With religion similarly. Religion
and Law are but symbols of Holiness and Justice. These
may satisfy our crude demands in this world of sense, but
the wise man will look behind the symbol for the reality ;
and obviously the reality Justice, the reality Holiness, are
not in our world. They have their being in the world of
Ideas. The good man and the just man, therefore, are
they who are sufficiently enlightened to realize (with
Shelley) that ' life, like a dome of many-coloured glass,
stains the white radiance of Eternity ', and that they must
look for the Radiance elsewhere than in the material
world.

Plato was a pagan philosopher, yet he impinges upon
Christian thought at many points. The Christian who
looks beyond the priest to God ; who declares Holiness to
be God and God Holiness ; who insists, furthermore, that

this world of sense is but a place of dust and shadow—that Christian has grasped (no doubt at another source) something of Plato's Theory of Ideas. God, that we can neither see nor touch, is an Idea. We can say, if we will, he exists only in the imagination of believers. Or on the other hand we can say that God *really* exists in a spiritual sphere more real than anything we know through the senses. To a Blake, a Joan of Arc, a Swedenborg, God and his angels are more real than any physical presences about us.

The plain man can understand a good deal of this, and he can appreciate that metaphysics stands in close relation to spiritual problems. But it is more difficult for him to see any practical purpose in the extension of metaphysics to all the phenomena and problems of everyday life. Yet we agree that a Society founded upon true Justice is a desirable thing, and we cannot afford to be impatient when Plato sets out at length in the *Republic* to discover how Justice is to be known and loved among men in full greatness and majesty. We need to understand the truth of Professor Taylor's comment, that philosophy was to Plato a living thing, not merely a body of impracticable theories. ' Philosophy is the *love* of wisdom, the passionate striving after truth and light which is, in some degree, the dower of every human soul. . . . It is the aspiration of the soul towards a complete vision in which its present doubts and difficulties may vanish. . . . Philosophy begins in wonder [and] Philosophy is, in Plato's eyes, a " way of life ".'

Plato's significance in world-literature would be grossly misrepresented if he were to be regarded as a mental gymnast and a profound thinker, and nothing beside. There have been other ingenious devisers of intellectual exercise, and thinkers perhaps as profound. It is not these abilities, unaided, that guarantee Plato's immortality. He was, as no one else has ever been in quite the same degree, a *poet-*

philosopher. True, he wrote in prose ; but his was the spirit of a poet—which can only be defined as intuition combined with an exquisite sensitiveness to beauty. Philosophers and scientists grope toward the truth ; poets leap to it. The process of patient examination through which Plato leads his interlocutors, step by step, is only his cutting, for the slow steps of pupils, a road toward the goal he had already reached by infinitely swifter means. At intervals in the history of thought and scientific inquiry brilliant investigators have found themselves drawing toward some conclusion that promised a new revelation ; but at the point of illumination it has been found, very often, that Plato too is there. Of the swift intuitive reach of poetry there are signs almost everywhere in Plato. The spiritual assurance, controlled depth of feeling, and majesty of utterance that belong to true poetry we also find in many of his pages, but best of all in the account of Socrates' death in the dialogue called *Phaedo*.

§ 6—*Demosthenes*

Given equal facilities, the tongue is mightier than either pen or sword ; and it is also far more dangerous. That oratory has lost its power and has now far less potency than it had as late as half a century ago, is no doubt due to our present destitution in the matter of great speakers, rather than to any lessening of human susceptibility to the wizardry of those who know how to play upon the emotions of an audience For oratory, at bottom, is essentially emotional in its method of appeal. It depends upon other factors than logic, or good sense, or integrity of motive. Many men who are intellectually and morally well-equipped fail as public speakers because they cannot use, or disdain to use, a technique which the Americans aptly call ' spell-binding '. Lincoln was a reasoning and completely honest man, but he was also a spell-binder. He knew how to give to his speeches that touch of emotional fervour which sways men's judgment whether their minds consent or no : '. . . That government of the people, for the people, by the people, shall not perish from the earth '—it is the cadence of the words, made a thousandfold more effective when spoken than when read, and not any assured soundness in the political philosophy it embodies, that has set this phrase ringing in idealists' hearts. But for other than immediate purposes oratory is definitely handicapped by the need of such an emotional supercharge, which must, in the main, come from the speaker's voice or gestures or from that quality vaguely described as personality. Printed speeches preserve only the husk, and some brilliant platform successes will not bear transcription in the harsher medium.

With these considerations before us it is more easily possible to estimate the genius of Demosthenes, whose traditional claim to rank as the world's greatest orator is unchallenged. The voice of tradition is, indeed, in this matter unchallengeable, since there is no standard of measurement available. The printed text of Demosthenes' orations can be studied and analysed ; the structure and the strength of reasoning and force of argument can be admired ; the evidence they give of unaffected patriotism and courageous devotion to the Athenian cause can in some degree be assessed ; and the occasional invective but general moderation can be noted. Beyond that, however, it is impossible for us now to go, so far as modern appreciation is concerned. We cannot know anything directly of what persuasiveness or passion or irresistible personal fervour Demosthenes added in delivery. Of such things we can only judge by proxy in the light of what influence he had on Greek history, and of the verdicts given when he spoke on indictments before a jury.

The glory that was Greece was waning during Demosthenes'

early years, of which we hear very briefly at first-hand in his most famous oration, *On the Crown*. 'I had the advantage,' he says, 'in my boyhood of going to proper schools, and having such allowance as a boy should have who is to do nothing mean from indigence. Arrived at man's estate, I lived suitably to my breeding : was choir-master, ship-commander, ratepayer ; backward in no acts of liberality public or private, but making myself useful to the commonwealth and to my friends.' The word here rendered as ' choir-master ' relates to the office of *choregus* (at the Dionysiac festival), undertaken by a wealthy citizen who bore the expense of the chorus for a dramatist's tragedies. We can gather from the references cited, and from what more we know of him, that Demosthenes was a complete citizen : a man of good education, a patron of the theatre,[1] a contributor to State funds, an advocate in the courts, a military strategist, a statesman.

By the time Demosthenes was about thirty, Philip the new ruler of Macedonia had embarked upon his campaign of conquest and was becoming a menace to Athens. Demosthenes, growing impatient of what he regarded as the Athenian leaders' spineless policy, came forward in 352 B.C. with the speech known as the *First Philippic*, counselling a rigorous campaign against Philip, and outlining practical plans for reconstituting the army and navy on what might appropriately be described as ' modern ' lines. Present-day readers, having no means of estimating the nature or effects of Demosthenes' delivery, are likely to be most impressed by his grasp of ways and means and by the level-headed precision with which he presents statistical and financial details as well as broad lines of national policy. In this oration he rebukes the assembly for its habit of muddling through, and in the *Fourth Philippic* delivered some ten or twelve years afterwards he still complains because they

---

[1] This was a duty, not a sign of mere benevolence.

allow the initiative to remain with Philip and act only when it is too late. Throughout the orations, the picture Demosthenes leaves with us is that of himself as a statesman initiating policy and plans which are approved in principle but not carried out with sufficient energy ; of an Athens which has drifted far away from its golden prime, needing time and time again to be reminded of its ancestors' pride and devotion both to their city and to the ideal of liberty for which it stood among the peoples. For a period he seems to have stirred a new something resembling the old spirit and fire, but once again it waned and the Athenians became still more supine. Philip died—murdered—in 336 B.C., but Demosthenes' hope of better days for Athens was checked by the conquering genius of Alexander.

In some respects Demosthenes appears much like one of the tragic heroes of the poets—a good man struggling against fate. His services to the State were valued and public thanks more than once accorded to him. Yet all his efforts could not save the State and as the times became more evil his personal enemies grew bolder. Among his bitterest rivals was another great orator, Æschines, who seems to have had certain physical advantages over him as a speaker. The two were in conflict at intervals for many years, but according to Demosthenes' assertion in *The Crown* Æschines was corrupt and a traitor, as well as being a carper who only came out of obscurity when, things having gone wrong for the State, he could blame those who had borne the burdens he shunned or even made heavier. On an occasion when it was proposed again to pass a vote of thanks to Demosthenes and to declare the award of a golden crown to him in the theatre for his public services, Æschines brought an action against the proposer, Ctesiphon, on the ground of illegalities in the scheme. The cause was not proceeded with by the plaintiff until some years had elapsed. Then, selecting an opportune time, he brought it into court for trial.

Appearing in defence of Ctesiphon, Demosthenes had really to defend himself, since he was the person actually attacked. This was the occasion of the oration known as *The Crown*, Demosthenes' finest performance in oratory. In it he surveys the state of affairs at the time he first became a public figure ; outlines the whole nature and foundations of his national policy for Greece, speaks of its ready acceptance ; shows its soundness and complete justification in principle ; and excuses its failure by the declaration that whereas a statesman's responsibility consists in the devising of proper plans, the issue and the end of all things is whatsoever the gods may choose. Æschines in his opening speech as prosecutor was not sparing in abuse of Demosthenes, and the latter's retaliatory passages effectively demonstrate how invective may be combined with complete self-control. We are shown Æschines as little better than a common adventurer living by his wits and never by ability. There are several references to his career as an actor—a shockingly bad one we are led to believe by Demosthenes' statement that the audience pelted him—leading to a summary comparison :

Contrast now the circumstances of your life and mine, gently and with temper, Æschines ; and then ask these people whose fortune they would each of them prefer. You taught reading, I went to school ; you performed initiations, I received them ; you danced in the chorus, I furnished it ; you were assembly clerk, I was a speaker ; you acted third parts, I heard you ; you broke down, and I hissed ; you have worked as a statesman for the enemy, I for my country.

In the end, the jury of five hundred Greek citizens delivered their verdict against Æschines and he was compelled to go into exile. How far the result of the trial was determined by the demeanour of the two principals we cannot tell, but this seems certain : that Demosthenes' case was helped by the blunt honesty with which he arraigned his opponent as a hypocrite, saying, ' What greater crime can an orator be charged with than that his opinions and his language are not the same ? '[1]   Above all, perhaps, the jury must have been profoundly affected by the references made to the glorious past when Athenians ' scorned to live, if it could not be with freedom.   For each of them considered that he was not born to his father or mother only, but also to his country.' Such passages from Demosthenes' oration could not justly be dismissed as empty rhetoric even by the most sceptical mind, for it is clear throughout his speeches that it was never his practice to say the things that men found it pleasant to hear, except when he felt that the pleasant was also the true.   On social subjects, no less than upon foreign affairs, he could be devastatingly frank, as when in the *Fourth Philippic*, in a passage curiously applicable to twentieth-century problems, he makes a plea to the rich on behalf of the poor, stresses the duty of the State to keep the needy from destitution—' There cannot, I believe, be found a wretch so hard-hearted who would be sorry to see poor men, men without the necessaries of life, receiving these bounties '—but also warns the poor against upholding causes that excite ' just complaint ' from men of property.

[1] Quotations from Kennedy's translation.

CHAPTER II

ROME

§ 1—*Ground Plan*

IN the sphere of statesmanship and government it was left for Rome to reduce to practice a large part of the Greeks' brilliant theorizing, and to institute an era of law and order such as the Greek States, with their unsettled conditions and fluctuating alliances, had not been called upon to establish. The contribution of Rome to the practical needs of modern civilization and the solution of its immediate problems is therefore incomparably larger than the Greek contribution, though in almost every direction where the yard-measure of utility cannot be applied, our chief debt is to Greece. The Romans had to accommodate themselves to what was, in one respect, the misfortune of finding that Greece had brought almost every department of great literature to a virtual perfection. The Roman writers might play variations upon particular themes—as they actually did, effectively and often nobly—but there remained little for them to do as originators. In epic and lyric, in the drama, in history, in philosophy, the high peaks had already been scaled ; while, in the matter of education, Roman culture had its roots almost exclusively in Greek soil.

Of necessity, therefore, as well as by circumstance and temperament, the Romans became transmitters, interpreters, retailers, of Greek literature and art ; and, as commonly happens in the processes of interpretation and retailing, both adulteration and dilution of the original are evident. The accidents which kept the Greek literary masterpieces from the knowledge of western Europe until a late century resulted in the vernacular literatures drawing upon Latin imitations and modifications of the original Hellenic spirit, with the result that there was for a long time a certain Latin fixation, as it were, in western literature.

Though idle, it is certainly tempting to speculate as to what might have been the course followed by the English Elizabethan drama if the sixteenth-century playwrights had happened to be as familiar with Aristophanes, Æschylus and Euripides as they were with Plautus and Terence and Seneca. Nowadays the balance rests the other way, and many who can reasonably claim to *know* the Greek dramatists' works only vaguely *know about* the Latin drama. Plautus (*c.* 250–184 B.C.) left more than one ineffaceable impression upon the work of greater masters than himself (Shakespeare and Molière among them), and his own work still has the power to interest and amuse. There are few forms of comedy in which he did not succeed, while it may not be stretching fancy too far if we speak of *The Captives* as the forerunner of tragicomedy, the type that Shakespeare perfected. Terence (194–159 B.C.) was less a man of the theatre than Plautus, and though his plays are, in all that concerns good writing, an ornament to Latin literature, they are probably less fitted to the rough traffic of the stage.

Lucretius (95–51 B.C.) wrote, in the *Nature of Things*, one of the world's really great philosophical poems. He was among those who anticipated some of the comparatively recent conclusions of modern scientists (the structure of matter, for example), but it is his metaphysical ideas that give the greatest force to the poem. Lucretius lived when the times were out of joint and he sought some compensating principle beyond the range of men of action. Both Lucretius and Catullus (*c.* 87–47 B.C.) influenced Vergil, and Catullus was himself a great lyric poet with a masterly command of simplicity, deep feeling and impassioned expression.

The *Commentaries* of Julius Caesar (102–44 B.C.) on the Gallic War and the Civil War have both an historical and an autobiographical value. They are especially interesting to our own post-war age, which has been flooded with the written personal defences and exculpations of military leaders, for (by comparison with these twentieth-century commentaries) Caesar's have an almost contemptuous air of detachment and indifference to others' opinions. He resembles an entirely passionless demi-god reporting a sequence of events at which he was present but in which he had no personal part. This complete impersonality might seem the negation of the true spirit of autobiographical writing, and yet in truth it conveys with masterly unconcern an impressive portrait of perfect competence and cold efficiency. There is never a question of *Was Caesar right or wrong?* but only a plain statement that *Thus Caesar did and thus.* Cicero (106–43 B.C.), whose life was almost exactly co-existent with Caesar's, gives a brilliant picture of civil and political Rome in that period, through his essays and letters, where the high principles of his public character are displayed in alliance with the natural warmth and friendly ease of his personal temper.

Nothing else can so well enable us to measure the greatness of Vergil's genius as an attempt to realize how impoverished (or at least how different) the intellectual and poetic heritage of civilized man would have been without the *Æneid* or even the minor poems of Vergil (70–19 B.C.). It was the smaller part of his achievement that he gave Rome her national epic, for in so doing he also enlarged the whole human consciousness. Yet though both Vergil and Horace (65–8 B.C.) were figures moving in a great world where history-making events were transacted, it is not easy to think of them apart from those quiet country contacts that account for so much we value in the poetry of both. Horace, indeed—however sophisticated in his writings, however much a hardened man

of the world incapable of illusion—lives in our minds as the
contented occupant of that farm in the Sabine Hills given
to him by Maecenas. There, writing his *Odes*, he would
compare new times with old and lament the growth of
artifice, even when

> violets blue
> And myrtle's fragrance, and flower scents untold,
> Will scatter sweetness, where of old
> The owner olives grew.[1]

The enjoyment of gaudy splendours, he frequently suggests,
is an ill substitute for the simple satisfaction of a life of honest
labour. 'What perfectly renders the temper calm ? ' he
asks ; ' honour, or enticing lucre, or a secret passage and
the path of an unnoticed life ? ' [2] Yet no man could be
less ascetic than Horace. He drank deep from the cup
of experience, and the taste of its dregs supplies a bitter
residue in the *Satires* and in such *Odes* as *To a Beauty
Faded*.[3]

Livy's *History of Rome* is practically the last great monument of Latin literature in the Golden Age. What remains
to us is only a fragment (thirty-five books out of a hundred
and forty-two), though in itself it is a very considerable
fragment that puts Livy (59 B.C.–A.D. 19) at once among the
half-dozen greatest historians. Through his work he is a
distinct personality to us, and his narrative displays an acute
dramatic ability and a fine sense of character.

An age which included among its writers Ovid (43 B.C.–
A.D. 18), Lucan (A.D. 39–65), Juvenal (A.D. *c.* 42–*c.* 125),
Seneca (5 B.C.–A.D. 65) and Tacitus (*c.* A.D. 54–120) can only
be regarded as minor when it follows upon a period of super-
abundant genius. In that sense alone can the term ' minor '
be applied to the Silver Age of Latin literature, which

---

[1] *Odes :* Book II, XV, Marshall's translation.   [2] Epistle XVIII.
[3] Book I, XXV.

certainly produced no writers comparable to Vergil, Cicero
and Horace, though in the *Annals* and in the *Agricola* and
Germania Tacitus is as great as Livy.   Ovid stands alone
as the poet of sensual experience in his *Art of Love*, while his
Metamorphoses is a rich storehouse of versified stories and
fables.   Seneca (5 B.C.–A.D. 65) stands in the curious position
of having inspired the drama of England, Italy and France
up to as late as the eighteenth century, though his own
tragedies seem to us to be wholly static and rhetorical.
They have nothing of the movement, flexibility and fire
we look for in poetic drama.   Among the later Latin
philosophical writings the *Meditations* of Marcus Aurelius
(A.D. 121–180) are outstanding.   The Roman Emperor took
over and documented the Stoic philosophy taught in Athens
much earlier by a freed Greek slave, Zeno (344–260 B.C.),
and the interest of the *Meditations* is enhanced by their
extraordinary persuasiveness to the modern mind.   Stoicism,
like Platonism (to which it is in some degree related), has
never since been without its disciples, and it might be
claimed that both these philosophies offer a strong challenge
to Christianity to-day.   But it is unlikely that Stoicism (or
Platonism either) will ever appeal to more than a fairly
large class of spiritual aristocrats. Stoicism permits no
external props (' seek not external help nor the tranquillity
which others give.   A man then must stand erect, not be
kept erect by others ' [1]) ; it is exacting in its rejection of
face-values (' examine everything all through, what [life] is
itself, what is its material, what its formal part '.   ' The
safety of life is this . . . with all thy soul to do justice and
to say the truth ' [2]) ; it requires a staunch impassivity
(' How ridiculous . . . he is who is surprised at anything
which happens in life ' [3]) ; it demands inflexible fortitude
—' waiting for death with a cheerful mind '.[4]

[1] *Meditations*, Book III, § 5.   [2] Ibid., XII, 29.   [3] XII, 13.
[4] II, 17.

§ 2—*Lucretius*

Men do not, in general, love pessimists. But can anyone who reads Lucretius with a sympathetic understanding fail to experience toward that amazing genius a mingling of sensations which includes love, and something deeper than pity, and a stirring of the mind and imagination rare in its intensity ? The profound pity we feel at intervals while reading *Of the Nature of Things* is nothing like the impertinent condolence of a believer over an agnostic ; it is rather our response to Lucretius' certainty of conviction that all created things are but congregated particles of whirling dust holding together for a season and then once more blown apart down the wind. This dismal theory, considered simply as a theory, might seem either wilfully perverse or ludicrous ; it is accompanied in Lucretius' poetry, however, by a variety of overtones and undertones—emotional and metaphysical—that transform it to a noble vision of pure unterrified despair. Lucretius may have been wrong ; no doubt he was. Yet he can teach us to face the worst with equanimity, if the worst should come. We feel drawn toward him in affection as we might to a frozen fellow-creature with whom we wish to share whatever vestige of warmth remains to us, not because he requires our warmth but because some quality in him opens our vitals. His picture of the end of life as an oblivion which is ' death's unvexed repose ' holds the infinite that lies in eternal silence and eternal night :

> Therefore, O man, by living on, fulfil
> As many generations as thou may :
> Eternal death shall there be waiting still ;
> And he who died with light of yesterday
> Shall be no briefer time in death's No-more
> Than he who perished months or years before.[1]

[1] Book III ; W. E. Leonard's translation.

Lucretius' desire was to banish man's strongest fear—the
fear of death and after-death—which is productive of
superstition and the endless terrors that arise therefrom.
His method was to build up an entirely rational theory of
the structure of the universe—but rational, in truth, only
from a given point. He regards the whole universe as compounded of ' atoms ' and ' void '—the atoms being held
together in varying degrees of closeness which determine
the relative consistency of all substances, whether gaseous
or liquid or solid. As the numerous direct references in the
poem show, Lucretius was a devoted follower of Epicurus,
who had himself been attracted by the atomic theory
evolved by earlier speculators. As the foundation of this
atomic theory (which in some respects was a brilliant guess
anticipating certain present-day scientific conclusions)
Lucretius postulates the existence of invisible primordial
bodies—' minim particles '—which cannot be destroyed or
subdivided, so strong are they in their ' eternal single-
ness '. These are Nature's primal germs from which everything else is compounded. If this theory is granted—and
Lucretius goes to considerable trouble to systematize it and
establish, as he hopes, that it cannot be refuted—it follows
that mind and soul are also substances similarly compounded.
Therefore mind and soul are subject to the same laws as
all substance. At death they dissolve into their primal
elements, as the body does, and are dispersed. Consequently
every terror concerning the hereafter is baseless : ' What is
there horrible, what so sad about it all ? Is't not serener
far than any sleep ? '

Lucretius' hatred of religion was due in part to the horror
aroused in him by the cruelties and excesses to which
religious superstitions drove men through fear or fancy ;
and in part to the natural antipathy of a tidy mind to what
is illogical and irrational. Religion, he says—citing the
case of Iphigenia's death on the altar at Aulis—often breeds

foul criminal impiety in man, as when that sinless woman was made a sacrificial beast 'to give the ships auspicious winds for Troy'. To root out the impulse that leads to such crimes it was necessary, he considered, to find a rational explanation of all phenomena from the beginning. His account of the formation of the world is a fine imaginative feat and one that is not far different from the speculations proffered in recent works based on modern geological knowledge:

> In that long ago
> The wheel of the sun could nowhere be discerned
> . . . but only some strange storm
> And a prodigious hurly-burly mass . . .

from whence

> Portions began to fly asunder, and like
> With like to join, and to block out a world.[1]

He proceeds to detail the whole round of creation and to trace the course of civilization, emerging slowly according to primitive man's increasing skill in satisfying his own needs. Stage by stage Lucretius builds up his rationalized universe, attributing every phenomenon to its (to him reasonable) cause—always with one end in view : namely, to teach mankind to look upon everything in Creation with 'a master eye and mind at peace', so that the world might pass from under the imagined dominance of omnipotent deities :

> O humankind unhappy !—when it ascribed
> Unto divinities such awesome deeds,
> And coupled thereto rigours of fierce wrath !
> What groans did men on that sad day beget
> Even for ourselves, and oh what wounds for us,
> What tears for our children's children ! [2]

It is always the discovery to men of 'the law behind' phenomena that is Lucretius' purpose, and though the world according to his plan may be far from benevolent, it is

[1] Book V.   [2] Ibid.

a thoroughly tidy one in which even the incidence of disease is accorded its rational explanation.

The innumerable poetic felicities in *Of the Nature of Things* are among its chief pleasures. Lucretius was a lover of simple things. At times indeed he seems to require no more than negative enjoyments from life—freedom from pain and care and fear. But if delights are to be added, the best are not those which belong to luxury and elaboration. More desirable than these is

> . . . to lounge with friends in the soft grass
> Beside a river of water, underneath
> A big tree's boughs, and merrily to refresh
> Our frames with no vast outlay—most of all
> If the weather is laughing and the times of the year
> Besprinkle the green of the grass around with flowers.[1]

Often in the middle of an argument which is intended to be purely scientific, Lucretius lights upon some image which at once summons up the world of living men and women. For example, we read the following passage in its context with the sensation that might be felt by a student in a perfectly-ordered operating theatre who suddenly saw a window opened upon a place of light and movement and gaiety. The poet is talking about colour diffusion in connection with his theory of images :

> And commonly
> The awnings, saffron, red, and dusky blue
> Stretched overhead in mighty theatres,
> Upon their poles and cross-beams fluttering,
> Have such an action quite ; for there they dye
> And make to undulate with their every hue
> The circled throng below, and all the stage,
> And rich attire in the patrician seats.
> And ever the more the theatre's dark walls
> Around them shut, the more all things within
> Laugh in the bright suffusion of strange glints,
> The daylight being withdrawn.[2]

[1] Book II.   [2] Book IV.

And again, when advancing arguments against the soul's immortality, he refers to those who shrink from death because they dread separation from life's lovely moments. They think the dead is wretched because, so they lament,

> Thee now no more
> The joyful house and best of wives shall welcome,
> Nor little sons run up to snatch their kisses
> And touch with silent happiness thy heart . . .[1]

—a moving thought that does not touch Lucretius, however ; for, he claims, we need spend no such pity upon the dead, since, after death, no remnant of desire is preserved. Even alive, Lucretius seems to have achieved a remarkable immunity from the illusions of desire. The long discourse on love in Book IV is almost cynical in its cold discounting of the snared lover ' eyeless with passion '. Love's symptoms, follies and joys are merely the entangling devices of Venus busy about her own ends. Therefore the lover attributes to the beloved beauties and graces she often does not in fact possess. And even if the beloved should be as beautiful as Venus herself, there are others equally so, and her actions may be no better than those of ugly women. In what he has to say concerning the need for the ' harmonies of Venus ' between husband and wife, Lucretius anticipates the ideas we now express by such phrases as ' blood-affinity ' or ' complementary sex-characteristics ' in reference to the successful ordering of physical relationships in marriage.

Lucretius' own life was not a happy one and his end appears to have been tragic. *Of the Nature of Things* closes with a section describing, in harrowing particularity, the horrors of a plague in Athens. It is a reasonable assumption that the poem (published posthumously) was neither completed nor revised. But the version we have, even if obscure in places and occasionally inconsecutive, is among the world's most engrossing masterpieces, the work of a great

[1] Book III.

poet and a resourceful thinker whose personality, though darker and more enigmatic, has yet something of the union of lovableness and profundity we associate with Blake.

§ 3—*Cicero*

Cicero is one of the few figures in the ancient world whose personality has been preserved to us in anything approaching fullness of stature. We know him in detail in both his public and private capacities ; we know him as philosopher, orator, statesman, husband, parent and friend. He was an idealist with enthusiasm for translating ideals into practical standards for the government of political, social and individual life. A reverent disciple of the Greeks, he took from them what was requisite to his purpose ; and to what he took he added that element of stiffening or bodily substance which distinguishes the Roman law-givers from the Greek formulators of the principles of right and wrong. The contemporary of Caesar and Antony, and therefore of Brutus and Cassius (whose passive fellow-conspirator he was against Caesar), Cicero shared in matters of State during a great period of Roman history, and he experienced the fluctuations of fortune that commonly by turns uplift and depress political leaders. Furthermore, Cicero has contributed as much perhaps as any Roman, or Greek, to the heritage which the modern world has received from the ancient. In earlier centuries he was important as a medium through which some part at least of the Platonic stream of influence was conducted into the main stream of Christian thought. At the present time it is Cicero in his personal relationships that attracts us most—through his letters, and through the *Offices*, a treatise (addressed to his son Marcus) setting forth Cicero's idea of what duties must be observed by one who wishes to live the good life. The idea of duty is central in Cicero's philosophical system, and therefore we find him insisting upon the need to subordinate personal desires to the welfare of society. Honesty, considered in a larger sense than by us, must be made the measure of happiness ; and honesty must control every desire and temptation toward personal profit or self-indulgence. There is no more powerful animating impulse in man than the passion for truth, and this it is that inspires us to seek after knowledge and the beauties of order and decency. Cicero lays down four main principles of virtue : truth ; social justice ; fortitude ; and moderation. Upon these corner-stones he urges Marcus to build. In particular, Cicero set a high value upon moderation as an article in human virtue, for he insists that ' no man should be so taken up in the search of truth, as thereby to neglect the more necessary duties of active life ; for after all is done, it is action only that gives a true value and commendation to virtue '. The *Offices* was written after Caesar's attempt to get the supreme power into his own hands, and considering the part that Cicero played in limiting this menace, it is interesting but not surprising to note how frequently Caesar's mistakes are cited to Marcus as a warning. There is a curious interest, too, in Cicero's views on the various trades and professions followed in Rome. Money-lending he regards, quite characteristically, as an unworthy business ; but it is amusing that tax-gatherers should be coupled with usurers as exciting hatred and ill-will.[1] Middlemen, also, are ranked low :

Nor are they to be esteemed as better than mean and ordinary people, that buy things by wholesale of the merchants, to retail them out again by little and little ; for what they gain is but a very poor business, unless they are guilty of abominable lying.[2]

[1] Cicero remarks in a later part of the *Offices* that it is the duty of the governors of a State to see that the people are not compelled to pay taxes.
[2] Cockman's translation.

According to present-day standards in such matters it seems inconsistent and snobbish that Cicero should regard fish-mongers, butchers, and cooks as ' pitiful and low ' and in the same category as perfumers, dancing-masters and others, on the ground that they ' purvey and cater for the satisfying men's pleasures '. On the other hand,

among all the methods of enriching oneself, there is no one better, no one more profitable, and pleasant, and agreeable, no one more worthy of a man and a gentleman, than that of maturing and tilling the ground.

Husbandry, as we know, was at low ebb in Italy at that time, and in commending this occupation to his son, Cicero was no doubt thinking nationally and in furtherance of the Roman statesmen's desire to give a new impulse to agriculture. This section concerning trades and occupations brings us closer to the standpoint of the time than do the observations on philosophical and abstract matters. Only in a limited sense can we speak at all of ' abstract matters ' where Cicero is concerned, since he rarely fails to bring abstractions into relation with practical affairs. For instance, he is not content to commend honesty considered simply as a general policy. Special problems arise concerning what is the honest and what the dishonest course in definite circumstances. He states the case of a merchant who brought corn from Alexandria to Rhodes when it was scarce and dear at the latter place and the Rhodians were prepared to pay a high price for it. Should the merchant sell the corn for as much as he can get, or should he let the customers know that there is now a glut of corn in Egypt and many shiploads are on their way from Alexandria ? Cicero at this point employs his favourite dialogue method (learnt from Plato) so that both sides may be heard. One speaker, Antipater, has no doubt that the merchant should acquaint his customers with the true position of the wheat market

and bear the monetary loss caused by a lower selling-rate.
But

Diogenes perhaps will reply to him thus : ' It is one thing to conceal,
and another not to tell ; nor can I be said to conceal from you now,
though I do not tell you, what the nature and essence of the gods is,
and what the happiness and chief good of men ; things which it would
do one much more kindness to know, than that corn will be cheaper,
because great quantities are likely to be here shortly.   But if anything
be profitable for you to hear, it is none of my duty to come and tell
it you immediately.'—' Nay, but you will find that it is your duty,'
may the other reply, ' if you will please but to remember that there
is such a kind of thing as a mutual relation and society amongst all
men.'—' Well, I do remember it,' may the other reply again ; ' but,
I pray you, is that society of such a nature, as that no man who lives
in it must have anything that is his own ?   If this be so, then there
is no more selling, but we must even give everything away that we have.'

Cicero declares, after putting another case, that the customer
should be told, and that traders who conceal such facts are
a ' shifting, sly, cunning, deceitful, roguish, crafty, foxish,
juggling kind of fellows ', a pleasantly resourceful and
emphatic gathering of epithets that leaves no room to doubt
his opinion.

The private letters of this Roman statesman and firm
moralist include a number written to his wife Terentia while
he was in exile, and it is evident from these that his counsels
of fortitude did not always govern his own bearing in
adversity.   In correspondence with others, Cicero ranges at
large between the trivial and the sublime, writing to one
concerning a disorder in his bowels and the purchase of
certain sculptures ; to another of the opening of a new
theatre ; to a third, lengthily, of the course of events in
Rome ; to yet another, notifying that he has renounced
sweet wines, olives and sausages.   Among the most interesting are Cicero's letters to Caius Cassius after the death of
Caesar, declaring that the assassination had failed to achieve
the conspirators' purpose inasmuch as the republic is still

in disorder and under a worse tyrant, Marc Antony. To
Trebonius he writes in despondency, and expresses regret
that Antony was not killed along with Caesar. The
historical interest of this particular letter is in the fact that
Trebonius was detailed to engage Antony in conversation
at the door of the senate house, so that he might be kept out
of harm's way while the rest struck down Julius Caesar.
Though the intimate personal letters of Cicero to Atticus
and others are as delightfully informal and entertaining as
any in the world, even these cannot hold our minds from
turning back to the historical letters with continuously
re-excited interest. In those we are provided with a first-
hand re-creation of the Rome we know at a distant remove
in Shakespeare. Cicero was a prime mover in stirring
events, and his voice speaks to us still, in tones far removed
from the frigid impersonality of Caesar's *Commentaries*.
And through the letters, we can see Cicero not only as the
great public servant we take him to be, but also as a man
among other men of corresponding stature who looked upon
him as upon themselves—as no greater than they, no more
remarkable, and with no more integrity than theirs. Others
among his contemporaries rated him higher, and in their
regard he was as exceptional a figure as he is in ours. Other
Latin writers excelled Cicero in certain ways ; he was not a
poet, and therefore he cannot be compared with Lucretius
and Vergil. But among the Latin prose-writers, at least,
he is pre-eminent. And because he touched life at so many
points, because we see him so fully and know him so well in
his own works, there is no one, even in Greek prose, that we
would unhesitatingly rank above him.

§ 4—*Vergil*

Vergil might be taken as a symbol of the continuity of
literature—for he is notably an inheritor of the Greek

tradition; and also as a measure of the wide difference between Greek literature and Latin. In the *Eclogues* Theocritus is Vergil's model; in the *Georgics*, Hesiod; and in the *Æneid*, Homer. But between Homer and Vergil there lies the gulf that separates *the literature of origination* from *the literature of imitation*. Only with careful qualification is it correct to speak of Vergil as imitative, for he had very considerable originality and creative ability. Homer was the fount of inspiration whence he learned, not to copy nor to imitate merely, but also to develop something new and great. To the lesser Roman writers, Greek literature was in effect a hindrance, moving them to preserve something of the form though perhaps little of the spirit. For the *Æneid* Vergil took hardly more than a germ from Homer. He knit together a different set of legends, sometimes with an Homeric reference, sometimes originating with earlier Latin chroniclers, but always unified and transformed by that Vergilian spirit which touches myth, history and national pride with the light of a lofty aspiration. The basic difference between the *Iliad* and the *Odyssey* on the one hand and the *Æneid* on the other, is that Homer's epics grew from a primitive soil, whereas Vergil's is from first to last a literary epic—the deliberate and designed work of an educated poet writing in an age of extreme culture. We are therefore provided with the contrast between poetry which preserves much that belongs to a splendid barbarism and poetry which is the direct product of a highly-advanced civilization. The love-story of Æneas and Dido is related in idea to the Greek story of Jason and Medea, but there can be no comparison between the temper of the Latin lovers and the terrible passion of the Greek.

Though Vergil lived through the period of civil conflict in which Caesar, Antony, Octavian and others were engaged, he took no active part in national affairs. Intensely patriotic and a true lover of Italy (especially of Italian

country life and of the sturdy virtues of the Italian peasants),
he was nevertheless a man of contemplative habit, shy and
retiring—characteristics which did not disable him, however,
from becoming the intimate friend of many prominent
contemporaries, including the Emperor Augustus, who
suggested the idea of a Latin epic. Vergil's aim in the
Æneid was to provide for the Romans—as Homer centuries
earlier provided for the Greeks—an heroic account of their
ancestry. The Romans had no very prolonged ancestral
record, nor any rich attachment of myth and legend grafted
upon their history. The old legend of Romulus and Remus
was not a particularly exalted affair. What Vergil required
was a story to stimulate national pride in the Romans.
Since the two great warrior peoples in literary tradition
were the Greeks and the Trojans, Vergil determined to give
his magnificent poetic frame to a story tracing back the
ancestry of Rome to the latter. In Greek legend Æneas
was the son of Anchises and Aphrodite. According to
Vergil, Æneas after the fall of Troy voyaged westward for
seven years, and at length landed in North Africa, where
Dido Queen of Carthage fell in love with him ; but Æneas,
warned by the gods, declined to remain with her, and Dido
killed herself. Afterward Æneas reached the western coast
of Italy, where, visiting the Sibyl's cave, he sought entrance
to the underworld to visit Anchises, who revealed to his son
the future glory of the race he was to establish. Returning
from Elysium to earth, Æneas journeyed to the mouth of
the Tiber, up which he sailed to Latium, the country of the
Latins, and there after a long campaign against enemies
raised up by Juno, he married the king's daughter Lavinia
and founded the city which was to become Rome, though these
culminating episodes are only foreshadowed in the *Æneid*.

Thus reduced to its thinnest and barest outline, the
argument of the *Æneid* no more represents Vergil's poetic
achievement than a skeleton in an anatomical laboratory

represents the loveliness of Helen of Troy. But even a summary does at least remind us that Vergil's creative resource was greater than that of Homer, if we accept the theory that the *Iliad* was the product of slow accretion and enlargement through many generations. Vergil had to be his own sole artificer ; more than that, he had to assemble the material which by his artifice he strove to shape toward a finished perfection. Artificer, rather than artist, is perhaps the proper word to apply to Vergil ; or, at least, he was as much artificer as artist. And in that lies his disadvantage in comparison with Homer. Homer's poetic beauty never seems other than natural. Artifice there is in Homer too, of course ; but it is the consummate artifice that becomes superb artistry. If we put the *Iliad* and the *Odyssey* beside the *Æneid*, we can see the perfect discretion and perfect rightness of the Greek watchword *No excess*. The *Æneid* has a rich ornateness that might be described as poetical finery—as though the poet were more conscious of the decoration than of the matter underlying it. This can be seen when Homer's description of the shield of Achilles is compared with the parallel passage in the *Æneid* (Book VIII) describing the armour forged by Vulcan for Æneas at the command of Venus. Achilles' shield *is* a shield. Whatever delighted amazement Homer's detail stirs in us is not accompanied by any feeling that the shield would be more suitable to a museum than to the battlefield. But the reader cannot feel so certain that Vergil realized Æneas' shield as an implement of warfare first and only secondarily as a magnificent opportunity for the display of poetic ornament. If it should be urged on Vergil's behalf that poetry *qua* poetry is a poet's foremost concern, we can answer that poetry must be judged by the effect it produces. The greater sense of reality and strength, the masculinity, which distinguishes the *Iliad* is an effect definitely produced by Homer's suggestion of closer contact with actuality and

practical knowledge of the uses of things. The *Iliad* is
rooted in the fullness of vigorous life ; the *Æneid* is the fruit
of intellectual resource. That is why some readers may
find Vergil's *Eclogues* and *Georgics* more satisfying than the
Æneid. On his farm in Mantua, Vergil was close to Nature,
and he had a deep first-hand personal knowledge and love
of its beauties, which he celebrated in the *Eclogues*. In the
Georgics, too, the patient labour and exquisite finish given
to the poems does not obscure the poet's intimacy with the
affairs of husbandry—crop-raising, vine- and olive-growing,
cattle-rearing, and bee-keeping—about which he writes so
beautifully. Agriculture and rural pursuits were at that
time in decline in Italy, and it was Vergil's purpose, through
these poems, to stimulate a new love of country-life and
occupations.

It is difficult not to regret that Vergil's choice of subject
for his life-work in the *Æneid* should have been as remote
as it was from his own knowledge and experience. Some
contemporary theme treated on the grand scale might have
given us much more of the spirit and temper of Vergil
himself—the Vergil who was at home with quite other
affairs than the clash of arms and imperial destinies. Even
as it is, the face of the peace-loving poet shines repeatedly
through the fabric of his elaborated verbal tapestry. The
similes in Homer come from a man with a special gift of apt
and precise illustration who is nevertheless completely at
ease among warriors. Vergil's images, on the other hand,
often seem to be accompanied by a sense of relief because
he can for a moment escape into the world he knew. The
Trojans pouring through the city gates recall the more
congenial picture of

> . . . ants that, mindful of the cold to come,
> Lay waste a mighty heap of garnered grain,
> And store the golden treasure in their home.[1]

[1] Fairfax-Taylor's translation.

Dido, distraught,

> Heard from the roof-top, through the livelong night,
> The solitary screech-owl's funeral song.

During Æneas' search for the golden bough which is to be his passport in the underworld, he and his companions enter a grove of aged trees where

> . . . The holm-oak rings amain
> Smit with the axe, the pitchy pine falls low,
> Sharp wedges cleave the beechen core in twain,
> The mountain ash comes rolling to the plain.

These are the things Vergil had seen and heard : these and

> . . . the creak of cables and the cries of seamen ;

and

> . . . new-born gales, that tell the coming squall.

The truth is, no doubt, that Vergil's greatness consists in his variety, which offers something to all men. If our mood is for the simple things, we shall find them ; if storied imagination attracts us more, we are given that too in profusion ; and a spiritual adventurer will discover, as Dante did in Book VI of the *Æneid*, a starting-place from which to begin the quest of all profundity.

CHAPTER III

FRANCE

§ 1—*Ground Plan*

ONE important consequence of the widespread Roman dominion was the difficulty experienced by other countries, after the disintegration of the Empire, in throwing off what threatened at times to become the petrified grip of Latinity. Even where, abroad, Latin culture had not sunk deep, it had yet saturated the administrative class and the upper strata of society. The prestige of Latin for all literary purposes was beyond computation. Its impress, however, was naturally deeper upon Italy than upon France, and deeper upon France than upon Britain. But whereas the early development of vernacular literature in Britain was interrupted and delayed by a series of national crises, French national literature went forward unchecked after its later beginning. Up to the close of the Middle Ages (from about 1080 to about 1500) French authors produced a sequence of troubadour lyrics, romantic stories of Christian heroism in narrative verse, variations on the Arthurian and cognate legends, chivalric love-songs and romances, and prose chronicles of the crusades (Joinville, 1224–1319) and of the wars between England and France (Froissart, 1337–*c.* 1400). The *Chanson de Roland* (*c.* 1080) and the *Roman de la Rose* (*c.* 1237, 1277) became part of the general European store of poetry in the Middle Ages. The *Roman* (begun by Guillaume de Loris) was enormously amplified and completed by Jean de Meung (*c.* 1250–1305), who made no attempt to match the spirit in which de Loris had started. On the contrary, he abandoned the courtly style with its queerly intermingled echoes of Ovidian

61

sensuousness and Christian chivalry, and used the second part (nearly nine-tenths of the whole) as the vehicle for a mass of realistic descriptions of contemporary life and the setting forth of a vast display of learning, yet tinged with a shade of something approaching intellectual independence uncommon to the general medieval tendency. Amid the numerous love romances, the perfect *Aucassin and Nicolette* stands out; and François Villon (1431–*c*. 1489) is unique because he somehow succeeded in uniting the gutter and the skies. There was scarcely any form of evil he did not master, but that did not prevent his singing like an angel. Presumably unlike an angel, however, Villon could never forget a revolting spectre waiting round the corner— Death :

> I know full well that rich and poor,
>   Villein and noble, high and low,
> Laymen and clerks, gracious and dour,
>   Wise men and foolish, sweet of show
>   Or foul of favour, less or mo,
> Of what condition, great or small,
>   They be,—Death (but too well I know)
> Without exception seizes all.[1]

One consistent feature of French literature has been the liking of its writers for grouping themselves into ' schools '. The *Pléiade* (Ronsard, 1524–1585 ; Du Bellay, 1525–1560 ; and others) set themselves to produce, in the national language, works that could be considered comparable with the classic masterpieces in Greek and Latin. The success of their endeavour was only hampered (rather badly) by their own intense admiration for classical models. What was needed as a complement if not an antidote to the *Pléiade* was just that roaring wind of robustious genius provided by Rabelais (*c*. 1500–1553). *Gargantua* and *Pantagruel* provide as marvellous an indication of one phase

[1] *Greater Testament*, XXXIX ; Payne's translation.

of the Renaissance spirit as Marlowe's poetry and Cellini's autobiography do of other phases. The escape of the human spirit from what seemed to be a prison had, as sequel, the unrestrained exercise of a wild range of faculties that exulted to excess in the new liberty. Though Montaigne (1533–1592) did not kick up his heels in the typical Renaissance fashion, his quietness of mind and expression served all the purposes of a complete sceptic whose one enthusiasm was for toleration. His *Essays* set the pattern for later English essayists, though none has been able to catch just the cool clarity of self-portraiture that is Montaigne's peculiar distinction.

The passion for precision of statement and a correct style, from which French literature has never since become wholly cut off, was in large part derived from the theory and practice of Malherbe (1555–1628) in his *Odes*. If to the influence of Malherbe is added the founding of the French Academy in 1629, we have the source of both the chief strength and the chief weakness of French literature for almost the next two centuries. Classic formalism and restraint are an excellent safeguard against imaginative extravagance and indiscipline ; but they also check the free ranging of mind and imagination and may, at the worst, encourage hardening of the intellectual arteries. We can only speculate as to what Corneille's future would have been if, after the triumphant production of *Le Cid* in 1636, no pressure toward academicism had been brought to bear upon him. As it happened, Corneille (1606–1684) managed to confine his oceanic genius within the narrow Senecan mould, and it is not easy to decide whether it was the greater miracle that the mould was not shattered or that the genius was not fatally crippled. His tragedies pulsate with an enormous intellectual passion, and the lightning of his mind plays about the eternal clash between destiny and individual desire. But if Corneille's achievement is a miracle, that of Racine (1639–1699) is, if possible, still greater. Not only did Racine work within the rigid classical conventions, but he did so without the slightest sign of friction between the matter and the medium. His *Andromaque* and *Phèdre* are tragedies of passion, in which the passion is somehow purified of its explosive element without losing depth or intensity. The frigidity with which Racine has often been charged is comparative only ; he is frigid in comparison with the romantic dramatists to whose work we are habituated in England ; but before we yield to the inclination to place Racine lower than these, it is worth considering whether some injury has not been done to our taste by a too exclusive familiarity with the hot spices of romantic drama. In this matter of ' romantic ' and ' classic ' forms it is interesting to observe that, if we English hold aloof from Racine, we show no disinclination to meet Molière (1622–1673) halfway, although he is as classic in form as his contemporary. The credit for this belongs, however, at least as much to Molière as to us, for while we lend a readier ear to fun than to catastrophe, Molière's range of acquaintance with men and women was wider, as well as more direct and less literary, than Racine's ; though Racine's understanding was possibly deeper and more penetrative. We may receive from Molière's plays the impression that he displays his characters more ' in the round ' than either Corneille or Racine, but this is an illusion created by the richer profusion of persons to whom he introduces us. There is a Molière ' populace ', as there is a (much larger) Shakespeare populace ; Racine has only a scattering of individual persons. But though Molière has *more* persons, he allows us to see only as much of each as is necessary to illustrate the theme or to justify the title ; he does not let his characters loose to live fully in the play as Shakespeare does : nor are they rooted in the larger life and business of the outside world as Shakespeare's are.

Molière's one clear advantage over Racine (and it is an inestimably valuable one) was his first-hand knowledge of the kind of people about whom he wrote, as compared with Racine's more literary and derivative knowledge of the Phèdres and Hectors; there is consequently present in Molière (discounting the primary differences of comedy and tragedy) that human warmth we miss in Racine, who was too complete a classicist to be a satisfactory humanist.

Among what may inclusively be called the miscellaneous prose writers of seventeenth-century France were Pascal (1623–1662) who sat down to write a religious treatise (*Lettres Provinciales*) and rose up a foremost master of French prose; La Fontaine (1621–1695) whose *Fables* are so much more than fables in their subtle delightfulness; Bossuet (1627–1704) who transformed graveside oratory into a fine art; Madame de Sévigné (1626–1696), perhaps the greatest of letter-writers; and La Rochefoucauld (1613–1689) and La Bruyère (1645–1696) who—the one in his *Maximes* and the other in *Les Caractères*—transfixed human failings and follies with arrows of wit and wisdom and truth.

Such eighteenth-century names as those of Voltaire (1694–1778), Diderot (1713–1784) and Rousseau (1712–1778) are an immediate reminder of the main stream of tendency in the literature of that period. Montesquieu (1689–1755) in the *Lettres Persanes* had used only a thin fictional veil to swathe his attack upon the government and Court of Louis XIV; and as the century proceeded and the evils of aristocratic oppression grew always worse, the spirit of discontent became more and more threateningly vocal. Bayle's *Dictionary*, 1697, came early in the general democratic movement toward intellectual and political enlightenment that was to be swept forward by the production of the first parts of the *Encyclopédie* just after 1751. For the furtherance of this enterprise Diderot enrolled the assistance of a small army of experts, and the Encyclopaedia became much more an instrument of philosophical and political propaganda with a clear revolutionary tendency than a mere repository of universal knowledge. Voltaire, in the early part of the century, had achieved fame and wealth as a popular dramatist. A period of enforced exile in England then fired him with admiration of English liberty and he set about a critical comparison of this country and his own in the *Lettres Philosophiques*, which were banned by the French government and publicly burnt. He was then forty. Some twenty years more were to pass before he was fully launched upon the amazing last period of his life when, between the ages of sixty and eighty-four, he became so voluminous as to seem like a literary factory, pouring out pamphlets which covered almost every department of literature, but mainly directed to the one end of undermining authority—both civil and religious. Religion in particular he hated, as much because of deficiencies in his own make-up as because of the vile crimes he had known to be done in the name of the Church. Except in a detailed study it is hard to decide from what angle to approach this human tornado. For his own age it was the cumulative effect of his corrodingly destructive criticism that was important; but, from amid the whole mass of his work, *Candide* now survives with intense vigour as a concentrated final expression of his attitude.

The something that was flabby and weak-kneed in Rousseau as a man is so glaring to us that we may be disinclined to give him the credit of being what he really was—a world-changer. How he became that we might see more clearly if his influence were not still so potent. He was the first of the moderns to preach the importance of the individual person—*any* individual person—in relation to the community : a doctrine which has been found acceptable probably because it is so flattering and yet carries with it none of the disadvantages the Christian conception of individual spiritual importance has for a good many. Rousseau's belief in the virtue of ' natural man '— man in his primitive state, untouched by civilization—is still attractive to people who feel themselves hag-ridden by the increasing complexity of civilized life ; and yet, viewed in a colder light, it is pathetically naïve in spite of the germ of truth at its centre. But when we have finished picking the mortar from the cracks in Rousseau's theories, we cannot deny him the right to be judged by the effect of his works. The vast edifice of modern humanitarianism has sprung from his foundations ; most of what ' the return to Nature ' has meant to literature stands to his account ; and he was one of the architects of the French Revolution—to what extent a conscious architect is less important.

No French writer in the nineteenth century recaptured the intellectual passion and driving-power of Voltaire and his contemporaries. The first half of the century was filled by the romantic movement, with Chateaubriand (1768–1848) as its guide to those uplands of the ecstatic imagination where the romantics breathe their natural air. Neither Balzac (1799–1850) nor Victor Hugo (1802–1885) seems quite as gigantic as formerly, though Hugo's poetry has worn better than his plays and novels, and as a poet he remains the outstanding genius of his time. There was, one feels, nothing he could not do—no power or gift he lacked—except the true artist's power of self-denial in his art. His novels should have been terrific ; instead, they are monstrous. Once he had opened the sluice-gates of his torrential literary eloquence nothing, except the final exhaustion of the source, could check what poured through —an inchoate collection of thoughts and feelings and aspirations and imaginings, with no distinction kept between the trumpery and the sublime. Still, the sublime *was* there, and when the technical restraints of verse (even though these had been loosened by the enlarging influence of the romantics) are present to keep him sober, Victor Hugo's genius runs clear. Balzac, a realist in intention, was clogged by a heavy top-dressing of shoddy romanticism. Realism and classicism have this in common—that, for perfection, they both demand to the utmost degree the stripping away of everything that encourages adiposity. In a sense, romantic art lives by distended outlines, which are the product of pleasant intellectual indulgences. But, in comparison, realism must keep to essentials—to the staple of life—and be content with a continuously frugal method —a kind of ascetic aestheticism. Balzac, when measured thus, begins to appear as less a realist than as a drab romanticist : a painter of life, it may be said, but much more a cataloguer ; yet his cataloguing was a deliberate part of his particular method and essential to its full realization.[1] Later critical opinion has elevated George Sand's peasant novels as better examples of true realism ; and the realistic novel was carried to a fanatical perfection by that ' martyr to style ', Flaubert (1821–1880). The reputation of Zola (1840–1902) has slumped heavily on account of the ludicruously disproportionate emphasis he placed upon the brutism of humanity. At the moment, three writers— Stendhal (1783–1842), Maupassant (1850–1893), and Proust (1871–1922)—are receiving more attention abroad than they had in France while they lived.

§ 2—*Rabelais*

It has been claimed in respect of many books that they provide a picture of the whole of life. That claim is never

[1] See § 5 of this chapter.

a very intelligent one—it implies far too much—but it
might be made for Rabelais's *Gargantua* and *Pantagruel* if
for any, and be more easily sustained for those conjoint
works than for most others. When we use the phrase,
' the whole of life ', we rarely pause to consider its meaning.
Life, to most people, means hardly more than the thin
trickle of energy they themselves experience : an over-
emasculate habit of living, which is no more all-of-life than
a suburban garden twenty yards by six is all-of-earth. So
far as it is possible to think of ' the whole of life ' in any
kind of comprehensible unity, we can apply to it only one
word—and it is significant that the word is Rabelais's—
Gargantuan. Rabelais's giant has just that incongruous
muddled heaving monstrous ugly profound shapeless leering
ridiculous virile gross abundant disorderly heap of qualities
which corresponds to life-in-the-mass. Because civilization or religion or education or debility or fear prevents
our taking from the mass more than a handful—picked
daintily lest we besmear ourselves—we have come to believe
that our handful is LIFE. The twentieth-century mind
therefore comes to Rabelais in a disabled and possibly a
permanently crippled state, and, thinking its disablement
normal, is disposed to consider this wild fecund creature
and his astonishing book disgraceful. The objections raised
against it relate chiefly to two factors : its obscenity and
its incomprehensibility. Obscenity can be of two kinds—
healthy and courageous, or diseased and mean ; the one
kind is accompanied by loud full-blooded (or full-bellied)
laughter, the other by a furtive snigger. There is more
laughter from the stomach in *Gargantua* and *Pantagruel*
than in any other book in the world ; and it could be
agreed that the stomach (man's centre of well-being) is the
proper seat of laughter. Dyspeptic people do not laugh,
or they laugh sourly and awry. And the smile of intellec-
tuals is only an educated version of the grin of imbecility.

The world is sick because it has grown ashamed to laugh until its belly shakes. It has forgotten that

> The Lord celestial
> Hath given enough, wherewith to please us all . . .

a lovely saying that comes from Rabelais himself. The world wants its flowers and its food, but it does not wish to be reminded that without the good services of dirt and dung it could have neither. Obscenity, like mould and manure, is ugly. But the evidence we have suggests that obscenity has always been a characteristic—major or minor according to the time—of humankind. In those ages, such as Rabelais's, when it has been acknowledged as one among a thousand dissimilar qualities in men and women, the world seems to have managed pretty well. But when, under ascetic stresses, obscenity (like nakedness) is hidden away—some being shocked by its existence while more snigger over its privity—the race is troubled as though by a hidden ulcer which cannot be kept from festering. Then ascetisism defeats itself, and turns a healthy natural animal propensity into a disgusting disease. Possibly the only book which has any slight resemblance to *Gargantua* and *Pantagruel* is James Joyce's *Ulysses*, which is, however, fetid with gloom, whereas Rabelais's work is disinfected if not sweetened with enormous untamed laughter. But obscenity, whether Rabelaisian or Joycean, will always be wholly and indistinguishably obscene both to the ascetic and the prurient, who, though enemies in principle, are curiously similar in their reactions.

The alleged incomprehensibility of some passages and chapters in *Gargantua* and *Pantagruel* is also a matter which depends more upon the reader's attitude than upon special qualities in Rabelais. If we have an affection for the savour of words, his massive catalogues will not dismay us. If we find pleasure in a meandering inconsequence, his

flights and excursions will not be baffling or wearisome.
Though it is a frequent lazy evasion to say that a writer
is ' a child of his own age ', it is certainly true that Rabelais
could not have been what he was if he had not been born
into the Renaissance period. Like many others in sixteenth-
century western Europe he was drunk with the sunlight of
the new day. He was brought up by and in the Church.
But he outgrew the Church. He studied medicine and
became a foremost physician. He was a scholar and a
teacher, but an enemy of pedants. He was a priest, and
yet a scourge of priests. A protestant unawares, but a
hater of Calvinism. Above all, however, he was drunk—
with words and laughter and that sense of enlargement and
release which made so many Renaissance men feel there
was no limit under heaven to the possibilities for human
expansion. Cellini is its symbol in Italy, Marlowe in
England, Rabelais in France. To them everything seemed
possible ; nothing was sacrosanct ; the desire for experiment was everywhere ; the abnormal beckoned them.
Gargantua was born from the ear of his mother Gargamelle ;
17,913 cows were required to provide him with milk ; his
clothing of blue and white used up linen and satin, damask
and broadcloth in ruinous quantities. This prodigality is
characteristic of the whole Renaissance period as well as of
Rabelais's imagination : again a symptom of the prevalent
drunkenness of mind and spirit in a generation which had
come, lean and thirsty, out of a wilderness. Gargantua's
horse is the size of six elephants : the sweep of her tail
mows down a forest ; the bells of Notre Dame are stolen by
the rider to hang at the animal's collar. Everything in the
book is on this scale of magnificent fantasy. Is it any
wonder, then, that Rabelais should feel the usual shallow
stream of words that suffices for the common vocabulary
inadequate for his purpose ? And so he pours words
about our ears until we feel almost swept away by them.

He tosses words in the air as a delighted child might blow bubble after bubble and send them soaring away into the sunlight. Not only words but languages also, as in the chapter describing Pantagruel's first meeting with Panurge, who talks in more than a dozen languages, known and unknown.

At the same time, it is all much more than a child's game or an intoxicated revel. Rabelais deals hearty thwacks at almost everything—institutional and otherwise —in the world of his time. From the midst of a riot of apparent nonsense we may find ourselves suddenly plunged into stark reality and the soundest sense. As a Renaissance humanist, Rabelais was of course saturated in the influence of Greek culture and idealism, and there are times when we catch not only the tones of that idealism but almost its very accents. After Gargantua has won the battle against Picrochole's men, he addresses the survivors :

> Our forefathers and ancestors of all times have been óf this nature and disposition, that, upon winning of a battle, they have chosen rather, for a sign and memorial of their triumphs and victories, to erect trophies and monuments in the hearts of the vanquished by clemency, than by architecture in the lands which they had conquered. For they did hold in greater estimation the lively remembrance of men, purchased by liberality, than the dumb inscription of arches, pillars, and pyramids, subject to the injury of storms and tempests, and to the envy of every one.[1]

Gargantua urged his son, Pantagruel, in a letter, to seek after ' virtue, honesty, and valour ' and ' liberal knowledge and civility ', adding that the very women and children aspired to the ' celestial manna of good learning '. Pantagruel became infected by a corresponding passion for the New Learning, so that ' the vivacity of his spirit amidst the books was like a great fire amongst dry wood '. That sentence can be exactly applied to Rabelais himself. He loses no opportunity of poking fun at pedantic extravagance

[1] Urquhart's translation.

of diction such as that used to Pantagruel by the young scholar from the University of Paris, an institution which had no love for Rabelais, no doubt on other grounds than that he liked ' the common manner of speaking ' more than the affected latinized language of the Parisians.

It is certain that the riches of *Gargantua* and *Pantagruel* are more evident the more familiar the book becomes. At first it is like a great mass of gold-bearing quartz thrown out from a mine. But as it is worked upon and examined by the reader's mind and imagination, the bright grains (and sometimes lumps) of pure metal shine out from the rest. The most typical thing in the whole book is the account of how Gargantua built the Abbey of Theleme, in which all the regulations of ordinary monasteries and convents were entirely reversed. It was sumptuous without and within, and Rabelais's architectural description is a remarkable piece of writing. Upon the gate was an inscription in poetry enumerating those who might enter and those who might not. Bigots, hypocrites, lawyers, usurers, kill-joys, and many others were to be excluded ; admission was to be given to the pure, honest, faithful, true, the gay and gallant, and the truly learned—as well as to

> . . . ladies of high birth,
> Delicious, stately, charming, full of mirth,
> Ingenious, lovely, miniard, proper, fair,
> Magnetic, graceful, splendid, pleasant, rare,
> Obliging, sprightly, virtuous, young, solacious,
> Kind, neat, quick, feat, bright, compt, ripe,
> choice, dear, precious.
> Alluring, courtly, comely, fine, complete.
> Wise, personable, ravishing, and sweet.

All the inmates of the abbey were to be most handsomely dressed, and the Rule of the Order was to this effect :

All their life was spent not in laws, statutes, or rules, but according to their own free will and pleasure. They rose out of their beds when they thought good, they did eat, drink, labour, sleep, when they had a mind to it, and were disposed for it. None did awake them, none did offer to constrain them to eat, drink, nor to do any other thing; for so had Gargantua established it. In all their rule, and strictest tie of their order, there was but this one clause to be observed,

DO WHAT THOU WILT.

Because men that are free, well-born, well-bred, and conversant in honest companies, have naturally an instinct and spur that prompteth them unto virtuous actions, and withdraws them from vice, which is called honour. Those same men, when by base subjection and constraint they are brought under and kept down, turn aside from that noble disposition, by which they formerly were inclined to virtue, to shake off and break that bond of servitude, wherein they are so tyrannously enslaved; for it is agreeable with the nature of men to long after things forbidden, and to desire what is denied us.

There, surely, speaks the voice of Renaissance humanism in one of its moods, a voice that was to be caught up, amplified and sentimentalized, three hundred years later in the humanitarianism of Rousseau.

§ 3—Molière

About the time that English drama was declining after its glorious efflorescence in Shakespeare and his contemporaries and successors, there was growing up in France an upholsterer's son who was to bring glory to the theatre of his country. The Jesuits educated him, familiarizing him with Greek literature and thought, though in the normal course he might have had no ready outlet for such acquirements. But young Jean Baptiste Poquelin (Molière was his stage name) was attracted by the theatre more than by furniture. In the year that the Puritans closed the English theatres (1642) Molière began his career as an actor. He attached himself to a company which fitted up a stage in the Paris tennis-court they had hired and started to produce

plays. He was then twenty. Three years later he went
to prison because he was unable to pay the bill for candles
used in the theatre—an eloquent enough indication of
failure. For the following decade he travelled with a
provincial touring company, and during that time they had
a successful and prolonged season in Lyons, where Molière
became known as a dramatist. He was called to Paris in
1658, and became Court dramatist, though nominally
Court upholsterer, in the greatest age of French literature,
when, under Louis XIV, Versailles was the glory of the
world in art, magnificence and manners. In such an
environment, targets for Molière's arrows of satire were
likely to be numerous, and no doubt the main types of
absurdity and vice were isolated in the plays he wrote :
literary affectation (*Les Précieuses Ridicules*), intellectual
pretension (*Les Femmes Savantes*), hypochondria (*Le Malade
Imaginaire*), meanness (*L'Avare*), hypocrisy (*Tartuffe*),
social climbing (*Le Bourgeois Gentilhomme*), the follies and
complexities of love and marriage and pedantry (*L'Ecole
des Maris, L'Ecole des Femmes, Le Mariage Forcé*). English
dramatic criticism must always be rather like the work of
spoiled children. Brought up on Shakespeare, we cannot
escape from what probably seems to foreigners the detestable
habit of saying that any given dramatist is less good than
Shakespeare. The happening of one miracle ought not to
incline us to belittle human achievements that fall short of
the miraculous. Yet even in literary discussion repressions
may lead to troublesome ' complexes ', and it is probably
better to clear the path by pointing out in what respects
' the French Shakespeare ' differs from Shakespeare. In
the first place he had the rather considerable handicap of
being neither a great poet nor a tragic writer ; which
immediately knocks away all ground for comparison.
Secondly, Molière was a social physician—liberal and genial,
but unerring in diagnosis—and his main characters are

' cases '. Shakespeare's characters were *people*, some of whom had happened in the usual course of human experience to become ' cases '. Thirdly, Molière was not much concerned in his plays with what might be taking place on the outer edges of the action. The characters were in a particular situation, and what was occurring beyond did not concern the French dramatist, though it always concerned Shakespeare. Fourthly, the fact that Molière was classicist in outlook and technique, whereas Shakespeare was romanticist, gives comparative sobriety to the former's work. But when we have said this to show that Molière was not like Shakespeare, sensible criticism will ask, *Why should he be ?* It may be true that he dealt with ' types ' and ' cases ', but at least he universalized them : they are much more than local exposures. As an observer of humanity he had the priceless advantage of knocking about in various parts of France and among various classes of people for nearly twenty years before he went to Court, and his plays are consequently set in a more extensive environment than they were likely to have been if he had belonged socially to the Court circle or had never been outside Paris. The English Restoration dramatists had most of the limitations from which he was free. They wrote plays with their brains, which happened to be first class. But brain is not enough. Molière brought to his work an infusion of common life which is as much deeper and more extensive than Congreve's or Wycherley's as Shakespeare's was than Molière's. Even ' cases ' have a human history and a background of average experience that colours all they do and say ; and within the limits of French classical comedy, Molière was a realist impressed by the dramatic possibilities of the life about him. His only really serious limitation, perhaps, is that there is not more variety of character in each play—that his misers and hypocrites and social climbers and affected young ladies do not get mixed up in company

with one another ; though if Molière had permitted them
to hob-nob together, the classical unity of action could
scarcely have been preserved. Had he lived in another age
and worked with the greater freedom of a romantic dramatist
there would undoubtedly have been a considerable gain in
flexibility of movement and design in his work. It is not
customary to see a number of pieces by the same author in
rapid succession on the stage, and the somewhat stereotyped
pattern of Molière's plays is therefore not generally apparent
in the theatre, as it is when two or three are read at a
sitting. He was, first and foremost, a writer of stage plays
intended to be acted. Their literary merit, high as it is,
must be regarded as secondary to the main theatrical
purpose they served and still serve so well. Molière lived
in an age of literary formulas, and it is remarkable that
within the confines of his formula he was able to achieve
so much and to make the repeated pattern of intrigue a
framework to carry a substantial weight of social satire and
criticism of personal follies and distortions.

Bringing an acutely sceptical intelligence to bear upon
his world, Molière detected a host of shams and self-
deceptions and polite artifices by means of which the
people about him held themselves aloof from contact with
reality. Madelon, in *Les Précieuses Ridicules*, details the
elaborate procedure to be adopted by a suitor and his lady
as a preliminary to marriage : he must utter inflated
phrases, be pensive, make his proposal in such and such
circumstances. ' Love affairs should be carried on according to good manners, which ought always to be followed in
true gallantry.' To which Madelon's father answers, in
sentences Molière would almost certainly have endorsed :
' What devilish nonsense is this ? This is nothing but high-
flying rubbish.' We know that the dramatist's castigation
of hypocrisy in *Tartuffe* brought the wrath of the Church
upon him (though that was well counterbalanced by the

king's increased favour), and his scarifying comments on other matters no doubt earned him as much disfavour as Bernard Shaw has stirred up in more recent times. Like Shaw, Molière was critical of doctors, and in *Le Malade Imaginaire* he causes Beralde to declare that Nature, given opportunity, will herself cure disorders that physicians' remedies may make fatal. Argan, the imaginary invalid, rebukes his brother for setting up to know better than the experts.

BERALDE. I don't make it my business to attack the faculty, and everyone at their peril may believe whatever they please. What I say about it is only between ourselves, and I should like to have been able to set you free from the error you are in, and, to amuse you, would take you to see one of Molière's comedies on this subject.

ARGAN. Your Molière is an impertinent fellow with his comedies, and I think it too much of a joke to bring such worthy persons as physicians on the stage.

BERALDE. It is not physicians that he exposes, but the absurdity of physic.

ARGAN. It's indeed becoming in him to set himself up to criticize the faculty. Here's a fine simpleton, an impertinent fellow, to make a joke of consultations and prescriptions, to attack the entire profession of physicians, and to bring on the stage such venerable persons as those gentlemen.[1]

Argan's objections were no doubt familiar to Molière, as denoting the attitude of those people he declined to accept as oracles without evidence of their authority. Sometimes, as in this play, he opposes pretentiousness with a cool and confident smile on his lips ; in *Les Femmes Savantes*, also, he ridicules with delicious gaiety finickingly educated and doubly-foolish women ; but in *Tartuffe* the laugh has died away and the smile faded. Cléante's speeches contain some of the most impassioned and exalted oratory in drama, and the sweeping magnificence of almost all Scene VI, Act I, alone prevents the selection of sentences to quote. Technically, *L'Avare* is an admirable example of Molière's

---

[1] Mathew's translation.

skill in handling a meagre plot within a fairly rigid structural framework. He brings freshness to a theme that promises little, and the characters are given a semblance of natural interest which is much to the dramatist's credit since they have little more than the function of puppets.

While English people get satisfaction from a conviction of Shakespeare's superiority, we have no dramatist between the Restoration and the twentieth century who seems anywhere near to having the ' modernness ' of Molière. Our modern blue-stockings are sisters of his ; our schools produce his affected young ladies ; the would-be gentleman is multiplied a thousandfold. He appears, in fact, more up-to-date than Shakespeare, for Shakespeare's characters have an emotional and spiritual stature above the reach of our own generation.

§ 4—*Voltaire : Candide*

In a life which seems to have had many turning-points, the three-years' visit Voltaire made to England in 1726–1729 was no doubt one of the most critical—as critical in the history of France as in the experience of Voltaire. Two years after his return, the *Letters from England* were published, and that conflict with authority which Voltaire had fled from France to escape began anew. It is difficult to imagine a condition of life and government in which those *Letters*, now seeming so mild and reasonable, could have been proscribed as seditious, and their author treated as a public danger. That this should have been so, is at once an indication of how far political oppression was carried in France at that time, and of the extent to which the contemplation of English constitutional liberties became part of the current of tendency which swept on to its violent outlet in the French Revolution. At a first reading, the

Letters from England are most striking for the wide range of interests covered. This is, indeed, a leading characteristic in Voltaire's works as a whole. His temper was strongly antagonistic to the assumption of an interest in anything as a matter of form, and it is because he was so intensely curious and had so liberal a spirit, that his books can still be read to-day with an extraordinary sensation of their unimpaired freshness. While in England he wrote about the several branches of sectarian religion, with a friendly eye to Quakers; about science, philosophy, trade, vaccination, poetry, tragedy, comedy, academies, and, of course, politics and government. He noted, among incidentals, that

No operas, plays, or concerts are allowed in London on Sundays, and even cards are so expressly forbidden that none but persons of quality, and those we call the genteel, play on that day; the rest of the nation go either to church, to the tavern, or to see their mistresses.

There can be little question but that the French authorities were fearful on account of Voltaire's references to the English parliamentary system. He was amused by the pompous seriousness with which the English regarded themselves, and he had no sort of illusion concerning the black spots in our history—the civil wars and religious persecutions. But he drew the inference that whereas civil wars had brought Rome into slavery, England had secured liberty thereby; adding:

The English are the only people upon earth who have been able to prescribe limits to the power of kings by resisting them; and who, by a series of struggles, have at last established that wise Government where the Prince is all powerful to do good, and, at the same time, is restrained from committing evil; where the nobles are great without insolence, though there are no vassals; and where the people share in the Government without confusion.[1]

[1] Letter VIII : *On the Parliament*; Morley's edition.

The implication suggested is that France, compared with England, was in a sorry state.

Letters from England came out nearly thirty years before *Candide*, and the difference in spirit between the two books is enormous. Voltaire tasted much of life in the period between. Affairs went from bad to worse in France, and everything tended to make Voltaire hopeless and bitterly cynical about man and about the universe containing him. *Candide*, a philosophical romance, is a literary curiosity— it manages to be so many different things, and to be almost entirely successful in all of them. It is a sort of spiritual pilgrimage, a diatribe against religion and oppression, a volume of fairy-tales, a congregation of awful horrors, a utopian novelette, an adventure story, a collection of critical essays, a philosophical pamphlet, a tract against war, a book of amours, and much more—all contained with ease and sufficiency in less than two hundred pages. By show- ing a total disregard for both possibility and probability, Voltaire also makes *Candide* a glorious extravaganza and a gorgeous parody upon the whole body of novels of romance and sentiment. Several of the principal characters die more than once—Dr. Pangloss suffers almost every possible form of violent death as well as being wasted by ghastly diseases—but whenever Voltaire feels so inclined he resusci- tates them and brings them once more into the story. The action moves with breathless speed from Germany to Bulgaria, Holland, Portugal, Turkey, South America, England, France, Italy and elsewhere; while running throughout is a constant stream of talk and ideas. Though there is so much else to claim attention, the ideas are of course central to the narrative. From the title *Candide*: *The Optimist* to the last words, ' All is not so well as in El Dorado; but all does not go so badly,' there is a torrent of cynical disillusion amounting to the most intense hope- lessness; and yet because it *is* a torrent, because of the astringent force of genius rushing through it, the book is much more invigorating than distressing, uplifting than depressing. The satire often runs to sheer fun, especially in the sayings of Pangloss the philosopher who, in the midst of the direst miseries and perils, asserts that everything in the world is for the best.

> ' It is demonstrable,' said he, ' that things cannot be otherwise than they are ; for as all things have been created for some end, they must necessarily be created for the best end. Observe for instance the nose is formed for spectacles ; therefore we wear spectacles. The legs are visibly designed for stockings ; accordingly we wear stockings.' [1]

Voltaire's terrible pictures of war are still terribly true— his fiction has been more than matched by our fact in the present generation ; and we cannot feel easy, either, about the persistent incidence of the disease contracted by Pangloss from Pacquette. In these matters the world has moved forward very little since the eighteenth century. Though discretion must be exercised in applying to the author himself the opinions expressed in *Candide*, we cannot doubt that Voltaire would have endorsed the words put into Anabaptist James' mouth : ' Mankind must in some things have deviated from their original innocence ; for they were not born wolves, and yet they worry one another like those beasts of prey. God never gave them twenty-four pounders nor bayonets, and yet they have made cannon and bayonets to destroy one another.' This doctrine of man's original innocence—the ideal natural man—was dominant in French thought in the late eighteenth century. It was most effectively propagated by Rousseau and was part of the philosophical background of the Revolution.

In El Dorado—' a spacious plain . . . bounded by a chain of inaccessible mountains '—Voltaire sketches his utopian community, wherein it is held that ' all men are by nature free '. The common pebbles of the highway are

[1] Morley's edition.

gold and precious stones, so that our ideas of wealth have
no significance there. Food is supplied abundantly without
charge at well-appointed inns. There are no law courts
and no prisons. Their happiness is such that, though the
El Doradians are a religious people, they have no need to
pray to their god : ' " We have nothing to ask of him,"
said the reverend sage. " He has given us all we want, and
we give him thanks incessantly ".' Nor have they any
priests or monks ' to dispute, to govern, to intrigue, and to
burn people who are not of the same opinion with themselves '. When Voltaire turns away his eyes from that
happy community, the actual world seems darker than ever.
In the words of one or another character he passes judgment
upon human malignity and evil in a multitude of guises.
Pangloss, driven to inquire why so strange an animal as
man was ever made, is told that it is none of his business.
The Turkish philosopher who speaks thus goes on to say,
in a biting analogue, that when the king sends a ship to sea
he does not trouble whether the rats are comfortable or
not. Earlier, Candide's friend, Martin, declares that ' the
poor in all parts of the world bear an inveterate hatred to
the rich, even while they creep and cringe to them ; and
the rich treat the poor like sheep, whose wool and flesh
they barter for money '. The cumulative effect of these
sayings from several mouths fixes the tone of the book, and
makes *Candide* one of the most tremendous indictments
ever framed against both the divine and human ordering
of man's affairs. That Voltaire should have been brought
to take such a view, enables us to judge the effect produced
upon him by the condition of his country in the pre-
Revolution decade. *Candide*, regarded apart from those
literary qualities which have given it permanence, is like a
distended ulcer upon the body of France. And remem-
bering, as we must, that the evils in a tyrannous constitution
had produced many other such ulcers in men's minds, it

becomes easy to see how inevitable it was that this accumulation of poisonous matter should find a drainage channel
before the State could recover its reasonable health.   Perhaps mankind is less dreadful than Voltaire pictured it.
Perhaps happiness does not turn to dust in the mouth.
Perhaps in the eyes of the deity we are something more than
rats in a ship.   But the great French apostle of freedom
had little evidence in the world about him that man and
man's destiny were other than he showed them to be.   All
beauty, all joy, all sweetness and peace turned to ugliness
and uproar before satisfaction could be had from them.
We shall not go far wrong if Cunegund, Candide's wife
after long pursuit, is regarded as the symbol of all life's
desirable things in the shape circumstances forced them
upon Voltaire's notice.   At first a pretty, innocent and
tractable child, she is buffeted, captured, outraged, made to
suffer every indignity and stain ; Candide recovers her,
loses her, finds her again old and ugly and horrible, marries
her because she expects it—and turns from her to other
lovelier and elusive women : 'We soon become tired of
everything in life : riches . . . ambition . . . the joys of
love.'   Candide develops an intense disgust : 'He was
ashamed to have walked in the steps of the wisest of men ;
and *he found women more bitter than death.*'

We cannot dismiss this Voltairean disgust with the
comfortable feeling that this too was a symptom peculiar to
eighteenth-century France.   Such disgust recurs at intervals
when the world is tragically awry.   *Candide* has received
more notice abroad in the post-War years than at any time
within memory.   It seems once again to be, in some
respects, an echo of things men know and of others they
fear.   Disgust has come down upon the modern generation,
and even Voltaire's small comfort is denied us : the hope
that possibly in the New World there are men of a nature
quite different from ours.   If there had been no second part

to *Candide*, it would have been possible to suggest that Voltaire's remedy for the evils of experience is to be found in some words on the last page of part one : ' Work, then, without disputing. It is the only way to render life supportable.' . . . ' Let us take care of our garden.'

§ 5—*Balzac*

Many attempts have been made by critics to determine what are the ' best ', the ' most characteristic ', the ' most important ' from among Balzac's novels, in order to help readers over the difficulty encountered in facing the huge mass he produced. But there is actually no way to surmount that difficulty, for the nature of Balzac is in his work as a whole ; and, since he did not live to complete the whole as planned, what exists—vast as it is—is only a large fragment. To say that *all* Balzac should be read does not mean, however, that he cannot be sampled with pleasure and profit. It is better to read one or two of Balzac's novels than none. But to get the full savour of him, it is necessary to do more than read him : one must soak oneself in him—a difficult undertaking because there is so much in his novels that it seems safe to skip ; and a reader merely in search of a story can quite safely skip. Balzac had considerable skill as a story-teller, particularly the gift of suspense, and the gift of being able to characterize a person with a few apparently hasty touches. He did not depend absolutely, as is sometimes suggested, upon detail laboriously accumulated. He used masses of detail, not because he was too clumsy to obtain effects without that aid, but because he felt—and on the whole rightly—that it was necessary to give to words a physical quality corresponding to the thing described. It is easy to say, for example, that he could have acquainted the reader with Madame Vauquer's

boarding-house (in *Le Père Goriot*) much more rapidly than
he did. Yet the purpose of those painstaking pages is
something beyond mere description, and it is impossible to
deny that Balzac does succeed in making the atmosphere of
the house, its inside and outside, eat into our bones before
he begins to talk about the people living there. To cram
the visual imagination was the least part of Balzac's intention, and readers have only to observe their own reactions
in order to realize how far the author succeeds in making
us responsive *through all our senses* as he places detail
beside detail and detail upon detail. There is no need to
illustrate this point by quotation. Let any one of his
books be opened in the midst of such a passage and the
process can be seen at work forthwith. If the book be
Le Père Goriot, each crumpled wine-stained serviette, each
maimed and broken chair, each garment, each of the
thousand objects introduced, down to the investigating cat
with its early-morning purr, is ' in the picture ' and contri-
butes something *to* the picture. What might seem to be
a disproportionate emphasis needs to be laid upon this
particular factor in Balzac's method, so that his readers
may be discouraged from hastiness if they wish to get what
Balzac strove to communicate. He happened to be an
accomplished story-teller, but not by story-telling alone
could he have succeeded in his intention to present *La
Comédie Humaine* through the long sequence of novels in
which he planned to explore large tracts, if not the whole,
of French city and provincial life. The Human Comedy is
less a spectacle to be noted from without than an experience
to be comprehended from within ; and Balzac does give us
an enlarged comprehension. His method, then, was sound ;
but his execution was frequently faulty. When he lifted
his attention from the particular to venture some sweeping
generalization, the result was rarely happy. He was a
natural realist with a strong taste for melodrama. We find

him entirely convincing when his eye is on 'the valley between the ridges of Montmartre and the heights of Montrouge' or, indeed, when his eye rests anywhere in the material world. But our confidence wavers before such reflections as that 'the chariot of civilization, like the car of juggernaut, receives but slight check when it meets with a heart less easy than the ordinary to break; presently it grinds it to powder and rolls on in triumph'. The reflection may or may not be right; the tone is certainly wrong. When the miser Grandet is about to wrench the gold-mountings from Charles' dressing-case—

Eugénie sprang upon a knife within her reach, and armed herself with it.

'Well,' said Grandet coolly, with a grim smile on his lips. . . .

'Father, if your knife does but touch the merest particle of that gold, I thrust this knife into my bosom. You have already killed my mother, and you will kill your daughter too. So now, go on, wound for wound.' [1]

The melodrama is magnificent, but again the tone is wrong. No doubt all unconsciously, Balzac gave a firm foothold for criticism of his novels when he chose La Comédie Humaine as their collective title. Reminded of the Divine Comedy, we realize how firmly Balzac was rooted in material soil, and how inapt he was at soaring; for the emotional heights he was somewhat broken-winged; the spiritual were completely beyond him. And yet the want of an assured ability to handle the greater issues is made less evident by the heightened effect Balzac could produce in passages of sentiment, where he employs a tender clarity that indisposes us to question the truth or otherwise of his creation. Véronique (in Le Curé de Village) has been deeply moved by reading Paul et Virginie, and Balzac observes:

In every woman's life there comes a moment when she understands her destiny, or her organization, hitherto mute, speaks with authority.

[1] Collins' edition.

It is not always a man singled out by an involuntary and stolen glance who reveals the possession of a sixth sense, hitherto dormant; more frequently it is some sight that comes with the force of a surprise, a landscape, a page of a book, some day of high pomp, some ceremony of the Church; the scent of growing flowers, the delicate brightness of a misty morning, the intimate sweetness of divine music—and something suddenly stirs in body or soul. For the lonely child, a prisoner in the dark house, brought up by parents almost as rough and simple as peasants; for the girl who had never heard an improper word, whose innocent mind had never received the slightest taint of evil; for the angelic pupil of Sister Martha and of the good curate of St.-Étienne, the revelation of love came through a charming book from the hand of genius. No peril would have lurked in it for any other, but for her an obscene work would have been less dangerous. Corruption is relative. There are lofty and virginal natures which a single thought suffices to corrupt, a thought which works the more ruin because the necessity of combating it is not foreseen.[1]

The picture of Véronique is a charming one—fragile, flower-like, virginal—but it remains a picture. Balzac *imagined* her; she is the creation of fancy; a painting in two dimensions only. When he is writing of men or women belonging to the types he knew thoroughly, Balzac can make a sentence do more than three hundred pages do for Véronique. Thus in *Le Père Goriot* :

The old maid Michonneau wore over her weary eyes a shade of greasy green silk, bound round with a piece of brass wire, which would have scared away the angel of pity himself.[2]

And in *Eugénie Grandet* :

Monsieur Grandet reflected profoundly on the smallest matter of business he took in hand; and when after a very long and full conversation, his adversary had exposed to him the secret of the pretensions he may have entertained, thinking that he had secured his listener, the reply he received was, ' I cannot decide until I have consulted my wife.' The miser's wife, whom he had reduced to a complete state of subjection, was in all matters of business, made use of as a convenient screen.

[1] Ellen Marriage's translation (*Everyman*).   [2] Collins' edition.

Balzac's eye for particular types of human character was as acute as were his eye and nose and ear for places and things. He could create or recreate men and women who had a strong earthly flavour or definitely-marked features of temperament and person. But because Véronique 'is a saint', all the literary power Balzac expends in *Le Curé de Village* fails to add the final suggestion of reality necessary to turn a two-dimensional picture into a living person. He was out of his depth with saints.

Balzac's greatness (and in spite of later critics' doubts he is indubitably great, when every deduction has been made for his faults and limitations) must suffer some belittlement under critical reference, inasmuch as comment tends to confine itself to single features and individual persons, whereas his strength lay in the multitudinous and multifarious. His books constitute a huge teeming world, though they are deficient in some respects we know to be essential in the world of experience.

When Balzac was writing, the full tide of romanticism was running in France and the flood fretted his foundations. If he had chanced to live half-a-century later while the realistic mode was at its height, he might have brought to that movement an infusion of variety and sanity that neither Flaubert's meticulous artistry nor Zola's sprawling fecundity could achieve.

CHAPTER IV

ITALY

§ 1—*Ground Plan*

IF the positive merit of a nation's literature must to some extent be gauged by the number of its great names and the range of its influence upon the world-mind, there are literatures that should be given precedence over that of Italy. Yet it would be merely foolish to suggest that the country which produced Dante, to mention no other, should be judged in terms of first, second, third, like a schoolboy's report.

There can be no doubt, however, that the great Latin tradition seriously retarded the establishment of a literature in the Italian vernacular, and even when such a literature was well advanced it was still an open question as to whether the Tuscan (Florentine) speech of Dante should or should not be received as the ' standard ' literary language for Italy. There had been at various times what might be regarded as competing literary centres in Sicily, Ferrara, and Naples. But, above all, there was the strong conviction in many learned minds that Latin and Latin only should be the medium for literature—a conviction that held sway in other countries also, but was stronger in Italy because of her closer ties with classical Rome. This language question was not thoroughly threshed out until toward the close of the sixteenth century, when the Academy was founded at Florence, largely as a consequence of the writings of Bembo (1470–1547), whose arguments in favour of the Tuscan language had the additional authority of disinterested advocacy, since he was himself a native of Venice and a Roman ecclesiastic. Thus did academic authority confirm,

after the lapse of more than two centuries, what Dante had
seemed to make inevitable in his own practice. It must be
noted, further, that the adoption of Tuscan did not represent a revolutionary breaking away from the Latin. Quite
otherwise, in fact, for it was through the Tuscan that Italy
found the clearest channel for the preservation of the high
dignity of Latin in combination with the invigorating
elements and flexibility of a living language.

Taking into consideration what has been said of the
language problem, it is not surprising to find the beginnings
of Italian literature lagging behind those of France by a
century or more, and when the quickening came it was in
part through the influence of the French romance songs.
Up to nearly 1300 the kingdom of Sicily played an important
part in the new literature (incidentally inventing the
sonnet), but then came, in the more northerly territories,
those precursors of Dante (Cavalcanti, Guinicelli, and others)
whose songs should not pass unnoticed because they sound
light in comparison with the full orchestration of the
Divine Comedy. Apart from these, there is the much more
notable Jacopone da Todi (died 1306), the Franciscan
mystical poet. Thus the way was prepared for the coming
of Dante (1265–1321), who was no more an isolated phenomenon than Shakespeare was. These supreme geniuses
found, in their respective times and countries, a ground
that was in some part cleared for them to work· upon.
Dante was rooted in the past—both the distant past and
in that which was less remote—and he came as the unifier
and justifier of much that, apart from him, might seem
wholly diverse and at variance. Though in the *Divine
Comedy* Vergil is kept outside the beneficence of divine
grace, the close attachment of Dante the poet to Vergil the
poet needs no pointing out : the poet of pagan imperial
Rome is the master of the world's greatest Christian poet.
Far more than Milton did, Dante utilized in perfect

harmony the full resources of poetic beauty and the full spiritual resources of Christianity in their majesty and splendour, in their remorseless penetration and justice and strong pity. And in Dante, for the first time in Christianized poetry, love sheds the external ritual and pageantry which makes so much medieval romance verse tiresome. It is true that the more profound spirituality of Dante gives the love element in his poetry an unfathomable profundity—a significance beyond the grasp of purely human relations, but no one questions that it is a truly divine significance; whereas in medieval love poetry in general and in many Arthurian writings, the semblance of divine significance often seems uncomfortably like an esoteric ritual devised by some fussily pompous pageant-master. Given the particular limitations imposed by medieval cosmology, Dante's theme goes, as no other poet's has ever gone, the whole round of creation in earth, hell, purgatory and paradise—of history and politics, of personal relations and of relations between God and man.

What Beatrice was to Dante, Laura was to Petrarch (1304–1374), both in his luric sequences and in his great unfinished poem, the *Trionfi*, which has a thematic sweep as wide as Dante's if not so deep. Boccaccio (1313–1375) has had the misfortune, on account of the *Decameron*, of being embedded in the English consciousness in the guise of an immoralist. He was so very much more than a skilful relater of pleasant indecencies that one must deplore the false puritanism which cannot get its eyes and mind beyond the thing by which it is disgusted. Boccaccio would be important if he had done no more than fertilize the minds of other poets to the extent he has done; but, in addition, the *Decameron*—one of the earliest masterpieces of fictional narrative—brought in that rich, coloured and lively representation of the doings of physical man (by which is implied much more than sexual man) which was needed to counterbalance a too definite preoccupation with man's spiritual destiny. Man cannot live by heaven alone, nor by an exclusive concern as to his heavenward path. Boccaccio and the people in his stories were healthy animals—*healthy*, as well as animals—and many of them were very much more than that. Though it is beside our concern to speak here of Latin works by Italian authors, it may help to correct any lopsided view of Boccaccio to mention his Latin poem, *Olympia*, which almost certainly inspired an unknown English medieval poet to write the lovely elegy *Pearl*, in which a father speaks in vision with his dead child in heaven.

In so rapid a survey as this, there is little need to name the large number of comparatively minor writers whose works fill the distance between the great fourteenth-century writers just mentioned and Ariosto (1474–1533), whose *Orlando Furioso* enlarged the scope of the heroic epic. This poem is a very remarkable achievement on account of its skilful combination of a natural story-telling ability with metrical variety and technical finish. And while he cannot be charged with wanton or irreverent 'guying' of the chivalric romances, Ariosto is refreshingly free from the pretentious solemnity which constricts most of those. He was a comic poet of the first order, a resourceful narrator, and an eloquent Italian patriot. Ariosto was also among the Italian dramatists who, about the turn of the fifteenth–sixteenth centuries, used Plautus and Terence as models in the production of 'scholarly' plays touched by local and topical references. More noteworthy, however, is the famous *commedia dell'arte*, a type of play in which improvisation was largely resorted to, with the vaguely defined action pivoting upon certain stock figures such as Pulcinella, from whom our Punch is descended. Machiavelli (1469–1527) in the *Prince* and the *History of Florence* enunciated theories of statecraft which are still an active influence in the world to-day, while a more engaging writer, Castiglione (1478–1529), employed speculations of a complementary kind in the *Courtier*, best described, perhaps, as a philosophical novel, though the passage of four centuries gives the book for us a good deal of the attraction belonging to historical romance. *Jerusalem Liberated* by Tasso (1544–1595) is among the world's great epics, and provides an interesting example of the attempts made in that period to bring Renaissance ideas and impulses into conformity with Christian doctrine. Meanwhile, the extensive speculations of Leonardo da Vinci (1452–1519), whose genius as a painter was combined with unlimited intellectual curiosity, had shown how far dogma and superstition might be questioned in the search after scientific truth and precise knowledge. The names of some of these pioneers are now scarcely known to us, but Giordano Bruno (*c.* 1550–1600) is remembered as one of those whom the Church attacked, as it did also Galileo (1564–1642), on account of those astronomical observations and conclusions which were the virtual foundations of modern science. Utopian literature is indebted to Campanella (1568–1639) for the *City of the Sun*, with its interesting anticipations of ideas commended by later sociologists.

Arcadia, the academy founded in Rome in 1690, held in leash a succession of lesser poets, upon whom was imposed a body of aesthetic doctrines and conventions by which the Academy hoped to check the poetic extravagances and flamboyant verbal gymnastics of Marino (1569–1625) and his followers. But, as usually happens when academies endeavour to fix canons of good taste, the result was merely the exchange of one set of conventions for another equally capable of absurdity. Experiments in drama in the early eighteenth century ultimately led to the production of *melodrama*,[1] plays in which the words were spoken to a

[1] A distinction must be kept between this melodrama proper (a simple kind of music-drama) and our modern application of the word to any play marred by emotional extravagance and false theatricalism.

musical accompaniment. It is possible to see the germ of modern opera in the melodramas of Metastasio, an Arcadian who transcended Arcadianism. But the outstanding personality in drama at that time was Goldoni (1707–1793), a natural comic dramatist who brought the Italian theatre back into touch with contemporary life, away from pastoralism and melodrama and the puppetry of *commedia dell'arte*. Goldoni in comedy and Alfieri (1749–1803) in tragedy held the mirror up to the life of their time in works which are as admirable for their literary and dramatic excellence as for their aptness as current commentaries. Alfieri wrote with prophetic fervour of a free and glorious Italy that was to come when the separate States should be united as a nation. The exalted vision which informs his tragic plays is matched by the barbed effectiveness of his satires.

It is impossible for long to dissociate Italian literature from the flux and reflux of political and national affairs. This close contact can be as plainly seen in Dante as in Alfieri, and in the latter's contemporaries and successors the clash of conflicting European destinies is predominant. The poems of Monti (1754–1828), especially, are full of echoes from the events in France during the Revolutionary period and from the subsequent exploits of Napoleon; while Manzoni (1785–1873), a romanticist, whereas Monti was a classicist, was similarly inspired in his early poetic period. But Manzoni's masterpiece is *The Betrothed* (*I Promessi Sposi*), an historical novel as fascinating in its subject-matter and noble in its treatment as it is interesting for the theories of historical fiction it illustrates. Manzoni held (as twentieth-century English writers of historical fiction also hold) that an historical novel should be a novel first and foremost: that is to say, history should be the circumambient air which is breathed by the characters, and the reader's sense of the past should be stimulated, not by the author's insertion of solid blocks of historical matter

grubbed up from ' sources ', but by the skill and subtlety
with which the act of re-creation is performed. So, in
reading *The Betrothed*, while eager attention is claimed by
the love-story of Renzo and Lucia and its interlacing
personal themes, the reader is breathing in, as it were, the
spirit of Manzoni's setting, which is Italy—Lombardy,
Mantua, Milan—in the early seventeenth century.

The growing-pains of romanticism affected Italian literature as they affected other literatures in the early nineteenth
century. One of the chief symptoms of the romantic mood
was the dark, picturesque brooding melancholy that Byron
brought to the last pitch of elaboration. But just as Byron
with his backward-looking tendency—now to the eighteenth
century, now to Greece or elsewhere in time and place—is
somewhat more than a pure romantic, so the Italian lyric
poet Leopardi (1798–1837) cannot be fitted wholly within
the romantic formula. His melancholy is deepened and
strengthened by a more than Byronic sincerity and penetration into the core of universal mystery, and his verse
technique has at its best a more than romantic coolness
and restraint. Mazzini (1805–1872), the great liberator,
began as an apologist of romanticism ; but, under the
influence of his increasing political sense of the need for
collective activity, he went on to deplore the excessive
individualism fostered by the romantic doctrine of the
paramount importance of the individual human soul. The
considerable literary importance of Mazzini's writings is
overshadowed by his influence on political action, and he
belongs to the world of affairs more than to the world of
letters. The last decade of Mazzini's life saw the coming
of the Garibaldian epoch, with Mazzini among the chief
architects of the united Italian nation. New Italy found
its voice in the poetry of Carducci (1835–1907), who
expresses the new national consciousness and also the anti-
papal reaction which was among its chief sensations. After

Carducci, we are immediately upon the threshold of present-day Italian literature, with D'Annunzio (*b.* 1863) as the most picturesque figure to foreign eyes and perhaps to many Italian also. In part through D. H. Lawrence's translations, however, Verga (1840–1922) has become well known in England, more for his short stories of Sicilian peasants than for his greater full-length novels. Among contemporary Italian thinkers, Croce has secured, in his own lifetime, a world-reputation for his theory of aesthetics.

§ 2—*Dante*

The *Divine Comedy* is either the greatest poem in the world or one of the three or four greatest. It is also, probably, the most difficult for modern English people to read, even in translation. In many respects it is a poem for all time, yet it is also of its own particular time—in regard to its intellectual and spiritual outlook as much as to its historical allusions and political references. If a reader's mind is habituated to the environment and circumstances of Dante's life, the difficulties encasing the poem fall away rapidly, though not wholly. Without some such preparation, however, the difficulties are considerable.

From the time Rome was captured by the Visigoths under Alaric in A.D. 410, culture became inundated by barbarism, except in the strongholds—the monasteries and convents—maintained by the Church. It is true that, in retrospect, much harm appears to have been done to humanism and the arts of civilization by fervent religious partisanship and the repressive weight of dogma ; but to whatever extent learning and art may have been compelled to serve religious ends, on balance the Church deserves far more credit than complaint for enabling culture to survive through the thousand years of the Middle Ages—for the

Church, like all institutions and all persons, should be judged at least as much by her best as by her worst. In one of her main endeavours—to suppress paganism and pagan ideals—the Church was sometimes tying down a natural safety-valve and closing an outlet of energy which had supplied much that was admirable and lovely in Greek life and art. Painters in the Middle Ages worked in chains : their technical accomplishment and imaginative faculty limited by religious subject-matter. The world's beauty called them—the beauty of landscape, the beauty of woman. The latter was spiritualized and allegorized a thousand times in the face of the mother of God ; while delight in landscape painting was exercised on *backgrounds* to holy families and on vistas seen through windows on canvases dominated by the madonna and child. Poetry, too—as we may see in sheaves of medieval lyrics—was often compelled to excuse its existence by some more or less uneasy partnership with religion. It is questionable whether Dante at first intended his early poems to embody that spiritual symbolism he afterwards traced in them. In the mass of troubadour love songs and chivalric romances we can see the veneer of Christian morality imposed upon pagan excitement and human desire. The conflict between these two elements is glaringly patent in the Arthurian romances, where flesh and spirit are not in partnership (the Church would have claimed, presumably, that no such partnership could exist) but at grips in a poisoned conflict. But paganism was not uprooted in those thousand years of medievalism, it was only throttled ; and when in the late fifteenth century, and in the sixteenth, the authoritative hand of the Church was tossed off at the Renaissance, the pagan volcano erupted— in the life and work of Benvenuto Cellini, in Rabelais's prose, in the poetry and plays and life of Christopher Marlowe. This conflict between paganism and Christianity has nowhere been better expressed than by Browning in *Fra Lippo Lippi*.

But the repressive tendency of the Middle Ages requires no demonstration in this modern period, when it is dwelt upon too much. What calls for emphasis is that there was another aspect—represented on its fleshly side by Boccaccio, and on the side of spiritual enlightenment by Dante, towering above lesser figures, and foretokening the Modern Age. In many respects, of course, Dante was dominated by medievalism. To the modern mind, the imagery in the *Divine Comedy* is often curiously archaic ; the geography of hell, purgatory and paradise often childishly ingenious. Yet Dante, too, was ' modern '—in the unstaling beauty and ambitious reach of his poetry ; in his nationalism and general political temper ; in his realization that the future lay with vernacular literature, not with the Latin ; and in his confident opposition to authority when authority seemed to him wrong. In brief, he stood (in secular concerns, at least) for the right of individual judgment against repressive authority ; he was a precursor of the protestant spirit maintaining itself with vigour against dictation from human sources.

Born in a time of political turmoil, Dante grew up in a Florence torn by the deadly enmity of the Guelph and Ghibelline factions—a warfare between parties such as Shakespeare glances at in the Verona of *Romeo and Juliet.* The feud had started in Florence almost a century before Dante's birth in 1265, a year before the Guelphs, to which his family belonged, re-mastered the city. He first encountered Beatrice when he was nine and, by his own account, never forgot her throughout the rest of his life, though at the age of twelve he was betrothed to Gemma, whom he subsequently married. There has been much speculation as to whether Beatrice was indeed a real person or simply an abstraction, a symbol of purity and holiness. The problem is not vitally important. It is evident that at an early age Dante experienced some spiritual revolution—

call it conversion, illumination, or what we will. It seems probable that he did encounter an actual person named Beatrice Portinari; but, considering his temperament, some other influence would no doubt have operated on him similarly if there had been no Beatrice. Dante was a mystic; and through some channel—it may be through a person, or through external nature, or through a more direct revelation—the mystic must find his path to union with the divine nature.

When Dante was eighteen, he began to write in honour of Beatrice in the *Vita Nuova*, a series of lyrical poems (linked by a prose narrative) describing his love for her. By his title, the *New Life*, the poet intended to imply the renewal or transfiguration of his life by the beatific influence of Beatrice. The *Vita Nuova* stands as a portal to the vast edifice of the *Divine Comedy*, and in the earlier work Dante's religious love mysticism is displayed only in a partial development. Beatrice becomes increasingly, throughout his work, at once a symbol and an assurance of his own ultimate identification with the Divine. Whereas, to most people, human love is a means to emotional and physical ecstasy, to the mystic spiritual ecstasy is the goal. The mystic tends always to objectify or personify: an impulse which leads a Wordsworth to consider all Nature the garment of God and a Blake to see angels around him. In Dante's *Vita Nuova*, love is far more than human sensation—it is Love the Lord—a Personage at one with the Divine. From the time he first encountered Beatrice—

Love quite governed my soul; which was immediately espoused to him, and with so safe and undisputed a lordship that I had nothing left for it but to do all his bidding continually. He oftentimes commanded me. . . .

Although Dante is, in important respects, a forerunner of the free spirit of the Renaissance and modern intellectual enlightenment, he was subject to certain superstitions of his time, and in both the *Vita Nuova* and the *Divine Comedy* the symbolistic magic of numbers is stressed, culminating in the greater work in a complex system of threes, and thirty-threes, which leads by manipulation to the completion of the whole poem in one hundred cantos, representing the perfect number—ten—multiplied by itself and symbolizing Beatrice, the embodiment of perfection. This web of numbers has no special importance for modern readers, except in so far as it permits us to see the almost mathematical precision with which the *Divine Comedy* is planned : it is in no sense a mere aggregation of parts, but, on the contrary, in form as well as substance, a completely finished work of art, of which, in translation, we may receive no total impression. The subject-matter used by Dante also shows how much he was, in particular instances, a child of his time. His cosmogony could not, in the nature of things, be in advance of current knowledge, and so the sequence of concentric circles forming the basic design of his universe is in harmony with Aristotle's conception, to which the medieval Church held with a rigid persistency against the later more accurate theories of Galileo and others. But it is somewhat startling to find Dante devising, with almost malicious satisfaction, a variety of horrible punishments in hell even for those whose offences we should sometimes assess as merely venial. To give overmuch attention to such points would be, however, to read Dante with too modern a mind and, perhaps, to underrate his inventive resources as a poet. The *Inferno*, by itself, must be regarded as one of the most stupendous feats ever achieved by the human imagination, and by this standard we should properly judge it, not by any modern ethical or humanitarian standard, Dante is, indeed, almost alone among the world's supreme poets in having no poetical ' message ' for modern readers. The metaphysical content of the *Divine Comedy* is incomparably rich; and so also is its poetic content—in language, imagery, classical reference and allusion, and original creative resource. But a profound metaphysic is not necessarily a ' message '. It is needful to be versed in medieval philosophy and Christian mysticism in order to approach Dante on this side.

What, then, can the plain man hope to get from Dante in translation ? He can get the pleasure of a magnificently narrated story rising on a sustained crescendo of poetic utterance, even though the latter element may be only faintly suggested in a foreign language; he can enjoy, apart from the main narrative, such memorable incidental stories as those of Paolo and Francesca and of Ulysses; and he may find delight and wonder in contemplating the marvellous reflected radiance of Beatrice, from the time she first appears to Dante and Vergil the guide, until at length the poet rises with her into the Empyrean and hears her say :

> Forth from the last corporeal are we come
> Into the Heaven that is unbodied light ;
> Light intellectual, replete with love :
> Love of true happiness, replete with joy ;
> Joy that transcends all sweetness of delight.
> Here shalt thou look on either mighty host
> Of Paradise ; and one in that array
> Which in the final judgment thou shalt see.

Dante then resumes the narrative :

> As when the lightning, in a sudden spleen
> Unfolded, dashes from the blinding eyes
> The visive spirits, dazzled and bedimm'd ;
> So, round about me, fulminating streams
> Of living radiance play'd, and left me swathed
> And veil'd in dense impenetrable blaze.[1]

[1] Cary's translation.

§ 3—*Machiavelli : The Prince*

Machiavelli's name and the adjective derived from it are often nowadays on the lips of those who associate his theory of government with a crafty low-down Jesuitism (what passes for Jesuitism among the uninformed). That interpretation has only one element of truth : Machiavelli did certainly hold that ' the State must be maintained '. But he did not hold that any means might be pursued to achieve the end. Only a blunderer could believe in such a doctrine, and Machiavelli was anything but a blunderer. He was clear-sighted, astute, concise and direct in expression, a lover of his country, and a hater of ineptitude. Much in *The Prince* is no longer applicable, because it was written as a manual for governers in an age when personal rule by force of arms was customary, and when conquest was a commonplace of politics. Yet outside the sections thus definitely timed there is so much timeless wisdom that for ' the prince ' could be substituted ' the prime minister ', or ' the president ', or ' the dictator ', and several chapters might be placed with advantage in the hands of those who endeavour to direct modern States.

Niccolo Machiavelli was rather more than forty when he produced *The Prince* (1513). He had had practical experience of statecraft as secretary to the Council of Ten in Florence, but both he and his country had fallen upon evil times when he turned in uneasy leisure to write this book, which is, actually, an impassioned appeal to Lorenzo de Medici, as the representative of a great House, to come to the rescue of his people and save Italy from barbarian dominance. If *The Prince* had been throughout a windy outpouring of patriotic or idealistic sentiment it would no doubt have been proclaimed for all time as a noble piece of exalted rhetoric. Exalted it is, and moving, rhetorical even, in the dedication and the final chapter ; but, in between, Machiavelli was concerned with the workmanlike performance of a supremely difficult job, which could not be done merely by eloquence or aspiration or the flourishing of banners. Even where it is old-fashioned *The Prince* is a fascinating book, because the reader is able to watch the author bending all his intellectual energies to the most impressive of all chess-problems, where the squares are States and the pieces armies and peoples. He draws upon the evidence of history, both written history and that in which he had had a personal interest—' a long experience of modern events and a constant study of the past '—for guidance in calculating what will be the outcome of the game if a particular move is made ; and, on the other hand, what move must be made in given circumstances in order to bring about the desired result. An injustice would be done to Machiavelli, however, if it were suggested that his pre-occupation with statecraft was mainly that of a player engaged upon an especially hazardous game of chess. Though he gives undivided attention to the player—the prince—he is far from indifferent to the fate of the pawns. From first to last his advice to Lorenzo the Magnificent is that of a counsellor who desires a ruler to be raised up to secure liberty for his people upon the firmest and most assured foundations. In the circumstances of the time—the troublous fifteenth and sixteenth centuries in Italy—the best assurance of true liberty was to be had under the rule of a leader strong enough to maintain peace and a settled way of life. Machiavelli was not a humanitarian, at least not a superficial humanitarian. He had no very good opinion of humanity as a whole. But who shall be blamed for that ? He argued from experience and the evidence of history ; he drew his general conclusions from the witness of many particular occasions. He believed men were as he depicted them, because he knew they behaved in that manner. In a word, he was a realist, not an idealist; a practical politician, not an architect of utopias. He was indeed impatient of utopists, saying that he thought it ' more proper to go to the real truth of the matter than to its imagination ' and urging that ruin might well lie in wait for the man ' who abandons what is done for what ought to be done '. It is easier for us to complain that Machiavelli's attitude in this matter was ignoble than to prove it unwise. If we searched history we could find no one better fitted to represent the opposite view to Machiavelli's than President Wilson, who, in our own time, aimed to rebuild the world on idealistic and noble lines. Wilson's tragedy was that of a pure idealist living in a world of subtle realists and blundering muddlers. Machiavelli would have kept in mind the necessity of considering the nature of the foundations before setting out to build a New Jerusalem; and if he had lived four hundred years later, he would assuredly have warned Woodrow Wilson in words from *The Prince* : ' A man who wishes to make a profession of goodness in everything must necessarily come to grief among so many who are not good.' [1]

While Machiavelli was certainly of opinion that the welfare of the State could not be secured by good intentions alone, but only by an exact calculation of what was possible in given circumstances and in relation to the known factors of human limitations, he did not counsel that the prince should comport himself as the weathercock of popular caprice. Though ' he must have a mind disposed to adapt itself according to the wind ', it was not the fickle and fitful wind of democratic approval. ' It is necessary,' Machiavelli acknowledged, ' for a prince to possess the friendship of the people ' ; yet in analysing the prince's essential qualities in detail in subsequent chapters, he leaves no room for doubt concerning what are the sound and what the unsound methods by which this friendship can on the one hand be

[1] Ricci's translation.

permanently earned or on the other hand temporarily purchased. The friendship of the people may, for example, he points out, be purchased by princely liberality—but to what end ? A time will come when the liberal prince's resources are exhausted, and he must then replenish himself by extortion and heavy charges on his people. Whereas if by the regimen of a proper economy he should at first earn a reputation for niggardly closeness, he will afterwards be thought more liberal ' when it is seen that by his parsimony his revenue is sufficient ' without burdening the community. This discourse[1] on liberality and niggardliness provides an instance of how extraordinarily up-to-date Machiavelli often is. Could anything come closer than this to the heart of present-day economic problems, when the princely liberality of governments has brought national resources close to exhaustion and heavy charges must be imposed upon the people to buttress the reputation for generosity?

Machiavellianism can be condensed into few words : It is the ruthless determination to seek and preserve the welfare of the State by taking long views. The ' great right ' is the end in view, and if ' little wrongs ' are necessary to achieve it there must be no shrinking. A pampered people will at length call down curses upon the head of a prince who has cosseted and flattered them to their own ultimate disadvantage : the surgeon's knife is swifter and better than the deferred and lingering pain which produces catastrophe or death. Some of Machiavelli's behests sound startlingly strange to humane people who receive advantages from modern States (or, perhaps, suffer disabilities under them) without ever inquiring into the machinery of statecraft. This, for example : ' In taking a State the conqueror must arrange to commit all his cruelties at once. . . . For injuries should be done all together, so that being less tasted they will give less offence. Benefits should be granted little

[1] Chapter XVI.

by little, so that they may be better enjoyed.' Slight
reflection enables us to realize that these dicta are still the
bare commonplaces of successful revolutionaries and auto-
crats, who, using a vigilant foresight, combine immediate
ruthlessness with deferred benevolence.

According to the standards of modern moralists who have
a sensitive nose for hypocrisy, Machiavelli is adjudged a
hypocrite. He did not find it possible to escape from the
conclusion that the human creature is half man and half
beast—the beast-half being part lion, part fox. The
rationality of a man, combined with the courage of a lion
beset by wolves, and the cunning of a fox menaced by snares,
constituted the necessary make-up for his prince. What are
accounted the primary human virtues, though good in themselves, must in Machiavelli's view be used with discretion by
those to whom is committed the paramount duty of maintaining the State. The prince will find it well to ' seem pious,
faithful, humane, religious, sincere ', and actually to be so,
provided that he can, when the welfare of the State demands,
change to all the opposite qualities and ' be able to do evil if
necessitated '. Before we condemn Machiavelli's hypocrisy
it is well to consider how far this same policy is pursued, if not
proclaimed, by civilized States in the twentieth century.

A large part of the pleasure to be had in reading *The
Prince* comes from the frequency with which epigrammatic
and quotable sentences are found, as : ' Time brings with
it all·things ' ; ' States quickly founded, like all other things
which are born and grow rapidly, cannot have deep roots ' ;
' Men change masters willingly, hoping to better themselves ' ; ' It is easy to persuade people of a thing, but
difficult to keep them in that persuasion.' On a particular
occasion Cardinal Rohan said that the Italians did not
understand war : ' I replied,' says Machiavelli, ' that the
French did not understand politics.' This might still be
said of the most politically-minded people in Europe.

CHAPTER V

SPAIN

§ 1—*Ground Plan*

THE situation of Spain, so far as language is concerned, is somewhat analogous to that of England. In both countries there is a tale of successive invasions which were impotent to impose upon the native speech the tongue of the conqueror. It is true that the Spanish language has a more definite Latin basis than English has ; yet, even so, it is colloquial Latin, and not official or literary Latin. The three centuries (5th, 6th and 7th) during which Spain was ruled by the Goths left no deep impress upon the language ; and the much more important seven hundred years of Moorish dominance are represented by Arabic additions to the Spanish vocabulary, not by any Arabic influence upon language structure. Without speaking of the provincial dialects current in the country, we may note that the main body of Spanish literature is written in Castilian, which (with Toledo as its centre) became the literary language of Spain, as Tuscan (centred on Florence) became that of Italy, and the East Midland dialect (of Oxford and London) that of England. Portuguese literature is, of course, as distinct from Spanish as English from Welsh, with the difference that Portuguese writings have been more widely disseminated abroad than Welsh.

To speak of the many authors' names and titles of works that claim attention in Spanish literature would make this sketch a catalogue merely. It is better to be severely selective and to mention only such as have obtained a more than national reputation. The beginnings in this instance are vague, and much must have gone before the twelfth-

century epic poem (by an unknown author) on the doings
of the Cid, that Spanish adventurer, Ruy Diaz de Bivar,
whose exploits have attracted the attention of numerous
writers outside Spain.   The first Spanish poet known to us
by name is Berceo (*c.* 1180–1247), a fertile producer of
rhymed religious narratives informed by a simple native
vigour and directness which sets them apart from the bulk
of similar contemporary writings.   But the earliest Spanish
writer of unquestionable genius was Juan Ruiz (*fl. c.* 1350),
the nature of whose work is characterized by the fact that
he has been called ' the Spanish Chaucer ', though on the
whole he is more uproarious than Chaucer, and in his wide
critical and satirical survey of fourteenth-century Spanish
people he displays a more vitriolic malice than Chaucer
would have found it natural to use.   But if Ruiz could be
vitriolic, he was nevertheless too richly human and capable
of broad fun to be meanly acidulous.   It may also serve to
place another eminent writer if, in contradistinction to the
Chaucerian Ruiz, we speak with suitable reservations of
Lopez de Ayala (1332–1407) as the Spanish Langland.
While Ruiz, like Chaucer, was prevented by the comic
spirit from a too desperate castigation of man's folly and
infamy, Lopez de Ayala, like Langland in medieval England,
writes in a mood of withering dejection as he contemplates
the disordered world around him.   Spain's outstanding
writer in the late Middle Ages was Jorge Manrique (*c.* 1440–
1479), who, writing exquisitely of the great human commonplaces, achieved a lasting reputation.   From about the
mid-fifteenth century onward there was a voluminous outpouring of popular verse romances on various national
heroes and historical figures, and also a number of ' border
ballads ' which, in translations of varying merit, have
become known to English readers.   By far the most prominent landmark in Spanish chivalric romance about this time
was the *Amadis de Gaula* (possibly late fifteenth century)

which provided a pattern for many other books of a similar though increasingly extravagant kind.

The invention of printing and the coming of humanistic tendencies associated with the revival of learning in the Renaissance period had begun to influence Spain before 1500. Passing over a succession of not unimportant dramatists (Torres Naharro, Vicente, Enzena, Rueda, and others) each appealing to a particular ' class ', we come first to Santa Teresa (1515–1582)—mystic, poet, novelist, letter-writer, practical religious reformer, and altogether a woman of outstanding genius—and then to Cervantes himself. Miguel de Cervantes Saavedra (1547–1616) had an extraor-dinarily adventurous career before he took seriously to writing. His father was a surgeon, and there is nothing unusual to tell of his early years until he became a Spanish soldier in Italy, serving there for five years and suffering a severe wound at the battle of Lepanto. On his way back to Spain in 1575 he was captured by pirates and taken as a slave to Algiers. After several ineffective attempts at escape Cervantes was ransomed in 1580. Returning to Madrid, he endeavoured to find an audience for the plays he had begun to write while in slavery ; but, the stage not being sufficiently profitable, he obtained employment in connection with the preparations for the Spanish Armada. Both before and after his masterpiece appeared he suffered arrest on different charges, and the issue of *Don Quixote* in 1605 seems to have done little to mitigate his financial and other anxieties. There is little need to restate the generally known fact that Cervantes' purpose in *Don Quixote* was to kill by ridicule the enormous popularity of the chivalric romances which had been in spate for so long. What he actually did was to create a little world of his own time and knowledge which affords a vantage-point, as it were, looking out upon a time-less and entirely unlocalized world. What men and women are in *Don Quixote* is, in spite of Cervantes' fantastification, what men and women will be, essentially, everywhere and always. The colour is the colour of sixteenth-century Spain, but the light is the light of the universe. Cervantes wrote poetry and criticism as well as plays and novels, but nothing else that he did approximates to the level of *Don Quixote*, by which alone he qualifies to rank among the half-dozen supreme masters in world literature.

The unique quality which has carried *Don Quixote* beyond the limits of time and place may be the better appreciated when it is realized that though, from some points of view, Lope de Vega (1564–1635) is the superior of Cervantes, de Vega's plays have not touched the universal imagination to anything like the same extent as *Don Quixote* has. Except as a name, indeed, de Vega is little known outside Spain ; yet he was a giant both in his positive achievements as a dramatist and in his influence upon the development of Spanish drama. Rueda, who died when Lope was a year old, brought what may for convenience' sake be called ' the common people ' into the drama, and thereby increased its range in comparison with the scholarly and aristocratic productions of the other dramatists up to that time. Lope carried the democratic and humanizing process still further and made the stage for practical purposes as large as life itself. Human types and social classes cease in his hands to be types or classes with special limiting characteristics, because they are all, first and foremost, *human*. As so many geniuses have done, Lope broke the confining bonds which theorists would impose upon literature, just as the contemporary Elizabethans in England were breaking them. He had something corresponding to Shakespeare's generous humanity and breadth ; something, too, of Shakespeare's sense of comedy. And, to his disadvantage, he had even more strongly than Shakespeare a sense of the box-office. He wrote to tickle the ears of the groundlings, but he lacked Shakespeare's marvellous ability to combine the highest ends of drama with the commercial process of giving the public what the public wants. Lope's tragedies are far from reaching the Shakespearian plane, and his greatest deficiency was in poetry. Perhaps Lope de Vega's fecundity was a fatal gift. The number of his plays is not exactly known, but it can hardly have been less than ten times the number Shakespeare wrote. He worked at an incredible speed and, in addition to his hundreds of plays, wrote a mass of poetry (epical as well as lyrical) and prose of various kinds. Lope's younger contemporaries included several important dramatists : Tirso de Molina (1571–1648), who was almost certainly the authentic creator of Don Juan ; Luis Velez de Guevara (1578–1644) and Juan Ruiz de Alarcon (c. 1580–1639). Luis de Góngora (1561–1627), another playwright, is more notable as the inventor of a highly elaborated (and much imitated) style in poetry, the structural nature of which can be best conveyed by likening it to the plague of *euphuism* that beset England round about the same period. ' Gongorism ' ran its course and was important in producing opponents as well as a host of posthumous disciples, whose excesses ultimately brought the mode into disrepute.

A considerable leap over many interesting writers brings us to Calderon (1600–1681), whom the rest of the world has come to regard as Spain's greatest dramatist, largely, it would appear, on account of an insufficient acquaintance with Lope de Vega's work. Calderon wrote much less than Lope, was much less resourceful, and was as incorrigible a borrower as Shakespeare, with whom he can be compared on only one other ground (and then at a distance)—his poetry, Calderon's one point of superiority to Lope.

Calderon died before the eighteenth century began, and since that time Spanish literature, from the foreign point of view, has been in eclipse. No useful purpose could be served here by indicating the currents of literary development and change in the last two centuries, during which

Spain has produced no positively great writer with a claim
to rank in world literature. In addition to such currents
as have a purely national interest, Spain has felt, in turn, the
force of the romantic and naturalistic movements which
were more potent elsewhere, but there is no need to particu-
larize the special minor symptoms which were apparent
south of the Pyrenees. In the present day, the brothers
Quintero (Serafín, *b.* 1871, and Joachín, *b.* 1873) and
Martínez Sierra (*b.* 1881) have had a vogue on the English
stage; while Vicente Blasco Ibáñez (1867–1928) owes it to
the war and the cinema that he found a large public outside
Spain for the *Four Horsemen of the Apocalypse* and other
minor novels.

§ 2—*Cervantes*

In any authoritative list of the world's half-dozen greatest
books *Don Quixote* would almost certainly be included.
The word ' authoritative' is a necessary qualification, for,
as far as can be ascertained by inquiry among English
readers, the book is one it is considered nowadays a duty to
read, rather than a pleasure. This is curious, because Don
Quixote and Sancho Panza and some of their exploits have
passed into the common currency of thought and speech;
and it is a pity, also, because the book contains many incidental delights aside from the main episodes. There is
something wrong with a generation that does not take to
Don Quixote joyfully; or, at least, there is something wrong
with that generation's method of approaching the book.
Cervantes was, after all, a champion of the average man,
and of the average man's standards and point of view. He
was a natural, free-hearted, unpretentious creature with no
literary or highbrow nonsense about him. He revelled in
another kind of nonsense—*Don Quixote* is full of it—the
jolly nonsense with which the plain man delights to

undermine the inflated solemnity of the pedant. Probably the inordinate length of the book and its discursiveness are handicaps in a hurried and harassed age, but it is impossible to imagine *Don Quixote* written briefly. A charming long-winded leisureliness is a part of its very nature, and should be inseparable from every memory we cherish of the knight's astounding and immortally absurd encounters. Its atmosphere is that of one of those summer days in childhood when the hours seemed to stretch ahead almost to infinity, inviting us to wander in the sunshine down any lane that opened up and to peer as we might choose through any hedge. Some such mood as that must be recaptured as we set out with Cervantes ; each moment as it passes must be counted for more than any end that may or may not be in view. It might seem to matter very little to us that *Don Quixote* was written to confound the pedants and 'to bring about the fall and destruction of that monstrous heap of ill-contrived romances which so strangely infatuated the greater part of mankind' in Cervantes' time. Yet the sixteenth-century Spanish author was in fact taking a hand in the necessary task that confronts every generation ; he was weeding man's intellectual and emotional garden that becomes stifled by the fungi of impotent learning and the rank, stifling growths of sentimentality. Cervantes might have gone about his business with a chopper. But he was wiser than that. Broken heads make martyrs. He chose instead to tickle the ribs of pompous dullards and romantic slobberers. The treatment was more than commonly effectual since Cervantes went about it with sly sobriety, not with a noisy guffaw. *Don Quixote* can be read, of course, solely for its happy ridiculousness and its surprising incidents ; but if full enjoyment is to be had, it should be read slowly and tasted fully so that all the quiet fun may have its chance. The *Author's Preface to the Reader* begins the game, as Cervantes deplores his inability to dress his book with the usual ' pedantic garniture ' of marginal notes, critical remarks, classical allusions and commendatory verses. The friend who is brought in to hear this complaint first tells him how easily such extravagances can be supplied, adding, however, that they are not to the purpose : ' Nothing but pure nature is your business ; her you must consult, and the closer you can imitate, your picture is the better.' *Nothing but pure nature* : that was Cervantes' standard ; that has kept his book alive ; and that is its value for the plain man who values the true above the false, the natural above the pretentious. But obviously the pursuit of ' nothing but pure nature ' might have led Cervantes into the bog of dullness, if he had not recognized that nature adores a sense of humour.

So much attention has been given by critics and others to the great moments in *Don Quixote* that it is a pleasant duty to insist that these are only moments, and that the whole book and every page of it deserve more careful reading than they normally receive. Wherever the leaves fall open there is something to ponder upon, some piece of glorious nonsense to enjoy. At this moment the opening is at Chapter XIX in the second part—*The Adventure of the Amorous Shepherd*. Don Quixote, as always, is mixing wild wandering absurdity with wisdom. He is talking about marriage : ' Marriage is a noose which, fastened about the neck, runs the closer, and fits more uneasy by our struggling to get loose ; it is a Gordian knot which none can untie, and being twisted with our thread of life, nothing but the scythe of death can cut it.' Accuracy may not be in that sentence, but profundity is. Lower down the page Sancho delivers one of his immortal observations : ' Many a man that went to bed well, has found himself dead in the morning when he awaked.' The truth is that *Don Quixote*, the book, is overshadowed by the characters in it, and we rarely get an opportunity of enjoying their surroundings as they deserve. Fools of genius are the rarest phenomena in literature, and Cervantes has given us two. It is in these sublime fools that wisdom and profundity seem to be found in purest essence. The non-fool is kept from profundity by the barrier of petty knowledge. In him the fount of primal wisdom is clogged. But the Perfect Fool is nature's mouthpiece, speaking without impediment and achieving spontaneous wisdom. In Don Quixote's poor brain the obstacle of knowledge had been nullified by too much reading of romances; the moisture of his brain was exhausted, he had lost his understanding and the use of reason. Robert Bridges speaks in *The Testament of Beauty* of ' this picklock Reason, fumbling at the wards '. Losing his reason, Don Quixote was no longer troubled by any such fumbling in his mind. He plunged into a world of vision where appearance and reality are not separated out. Life became for him a unity. He describes himself as the man ' who cannot be enchanted '; what he sees *is*. He can never be, therefore, a man divided against himself. There is no fumbling Reason in his brain to make him doubt the validity of his intuitions.

But the Don is a wanderer in time and space as well as in eternity. The people he moves among are real people, not figures in a romance but authentic Spanish innkeepers, country wenches, swineherds, barbers, curates, and a host more. What Dickens did for the life of the roads in nineteenth-century England, Cervantes in some sort did for sixteenth-century Spain : his book is a world in itself, alive with living things. Here is a lad on his way to the wars :

They now spurred on towards the inn, and soon overtook on the road a young fellow beating it on the hoof pretty leisurely. He carried his sword over his shoulder with a bundle of clothes hanging upon it ; which, to all outward appearance, consisted of a pair of breeches, a cloak and a shirt or two. He had on a tattered velvet jerkin, with a ragged satin lining ; his shirt hung out, his stockings were of silk, and his shoes square at the toes, after the court fashion. He seemed about eighteen or nineteen years of age, a good pleasant-looked lad, and of a lively and active disposition. To pass the fatigue of his journey the best he could, he sung all the way, and as they came near him, was just ending the last words of a ballad :

> ' A plague on ill luck ! Now my ready's all gone,
> To the wars poor pilgarlic must trudge ;
> Though had I but money to rake as I've done,
> The devil a foot would I budge.' [1]

In another episode we read that a woman ' gave a roll, and a couple of eggs, to a young noviciate of the church, who could write, and he wrote two letters for her '. By such means Cervantes gives to his book the sense of common naturalness that is its special virtue, for this quality would preserve it, even if the more prominent features were less praiseworthy. Yet how far beyond praise those features are : the description of the knight's rusty armour, with its patched helmet ; the rectangularity of Rozinante the horse ; the exploits and sayings of Sancho ; the adventure of the windmills ; the battle of the wineskins. . . .

A wise reader might profitably read *Don Quixote* afresh each year, spending time leisurely upon each page, drawing the sense and, we might say, the succulence from every paragraph. So far from being an overrated book, it is, on the contrary, an under-appreciated one—in present-day England at any rate. It will most certainly bore the hasty reader whose only object is to have done with one book in order that the next may be begun. Great literature, however, has nothing to do with the hasty reader.

§ 3—*Calderon*

With that disregard for positive excellence which sometimes marks foreign judgments of another nation's literature, England has for long regarded Calderon, instead of

---

[1] Motteux's translation.

Lope de Vega, as Spain's leading dramatist. And until a readily available translation of Lope is provided, Fitz-Gerald's version of six plays by Calderon will no doubt continue to serve as our most familiar means of introduction to Spanish drama. This limitation is unfortunate, but for the present it has to be accepted, and we must be content to find the pleasure and interest that are unquestionably present in FitzGerald's Calderon.

The best play among the six is *The Mayor of Zalamea*, though it shows Calderon's peculiarly unsatisfactory qualities as well as his merits. He appears to have had difficulty in giving his secular pieces anything like a uniform dramatic texture. *The Mayor* is strong drama, comedy, tragedy and one or two other kinds clumsily patched together ; the parts are good in themselves, but there is no effective unification, and there is no dominant mood. Shakespeare mixed tragedy and comedy ; but, in him, the two elements are always accordant with the mood to which the particular play is attuned. There is no possibility of the mood of *Hamlet* or *Macbeth* straying from the tragic level because the grave-diggers appear in the one and the drunken porter in the other. Calderon was much more casual : he seems to get his second wind, and his third, and so on, as the play progresses ; and it consequently develops in a series of dramatic gasps. This is disconcerting, because (again to illustrate from *The Mayor of Zalamea*) the sudden change of mood when Isabel is carried off by the Captain is not sufficient to prepare us for her violation ; and because of that unpreparedness the Captain's execution is still less acceptable. Furthermore, it is not established that the appearance of Philip II in the final scene was a dramatic necessity ; he serves as little more than a sounding-board for the mayor's village rhetoric as the local champion of righteousness and (somewhat rough) justice. These, however, are faults in construction and craftsmanship which need not interfere with a moment-by-moment enjoyment of Calderon's plays. The soldier scene which begins *The Mayor* is admirably 'alive', and smells authentically of life on the march and in camp. The dramatist's untidiness in his incidentals can be seen in relation to the two characters Don Mendo and Nuño in *The Mayor of Zalamea*, who have no vital part and no real function in the play. For their own sakes, however, we could wish to see much more of them than we do. They are, so far as dramatic construction is concerned, excrescences; but Calderon had evidently drunk deep of Cervantes and he introduces these two in the sergeant's words: ' Why it must be Don Quixote himself with his very Rozinante too, that Michel Cervantes writes of.' FitzGerald points out certain ' odd coincidences' between Shakespeare and Calderon. The one he notes particularly is in *Keep Your Own Secret*, where Lazaro the comic servant describes a fight in terms which, to our minds, are curiously reminiscent of Falstaff's encounter with the men in buckram. There is also in *The Mayor* a passage strangely like a variant upon Polonius' farewell injunctions to Laertes. Pedro Crespo, the farmer who becomes mayor of Zalamea, bidding good-bye to his soldier son Juan, says:

By God's grace, boy, thou cam'st of honourable if of humble stock; bear both in mind, so as neither to be daunted from trying to rise, nor puffed up so as to be sure to fall. How many have done away the memory of a defect by carrying themselves modestly; while others again have begotten a blemish only by being too proud of being born without one. There is a just humility that will maintain thine own dignity, and yet make thee insensible to many a rub that galls the proud spirit. Be courteous in thy manner, and liberal in thy purse; for 'tis the hand to the bonnet and in the pocket that makes friends in this world; of which to gain one good, all the gold the sun breeds in India, or the universal sea sucks down, were a cheap purchase. Speak no evil of women; I tell thee the meanest of them deserves our respect; for of women do we not all come? Quarrel with no one but with good cause; by the Lord, over and over again, when I see masters and schools of arms among us, I say to myself, ' This is not the thing

we want at all, *How to fight*, but, *Why to fight ?* that is the lesson we
want to learn ' . . . [1]

Calderon's gifts were literary rather than dramatic.
That is to say, his plays depend for their effect more upon
verbal and lyrical qualities than upon action and character.
Considering that this is so, his power of sustaining interest
is remarkable, and in such a piece as the *Painter of Dishonour*
the limpid and lucid flow of the dialogue and the easy
expressiveness of the lengthier speeches provide considerable
pleasure. The lyrism of many passages has been remarked
as Calderon's chief excellence, and in this respect his plays
have a closer resemblance to our own lesser Elizabethan
comedies than to any other. Occasionally the lyrical
passages seem strangely inharmonious with the predominant
temper of a particular scene—as in Isabel's eloquence at
the beginning of Act III in *The Mayor of Zalamea* ; but
even when it is ' out of character ' Calderon's lyrism is
nevertheless delightful to hear, and considerably less disconcerting than the manner in which he will on occasion
end a play with an almost impatient plunge into catastrophe.
It was, indeed, only catastrophe that he could manage ;
the inevitable and implacable march of tragedy was beyond
his scope. *The Painter of Dishonour* would, in the hands of
a differently equipped dramatist, have been a fine tragedy.
Calderon makes it no more than an extremely interesting
play which ends stumblingly in disaster, when the husband
suddenly shoots his wife and her kidnapper about two
minutes before the final curtain.

Gil Perez the Gallician has more continuous dramatic
action, and is an exciting piece of robustious melodrama
with a Robin-Hoodish hero. Gil's raid upon the judge's
apartment in order to read the indictment against himself
in the presence of the powerless judge is a well-managed
scene, and would be more so if Gil's escape were more

[1] FitzGerald's translation.

satisfactorily engineered. *Beware of Smooth Water* deals
with an interesting situation which is allowed to peter out
tamely, largely on account of Calderon's insufficient skill in
building-up and handling characters. The diverse tempera-
ments of the two sisters, Clara and Eugenia, are well stated
—so well that high expectations are roused in the audience.
Speaking in a room in their father's house in Madrid, Clara
says, ' I like its quietude ' :

> EUGENIA. I want the lively streets whose flowers are shops,
>   Carriages, soldiers, ladies, cavaliers,
>   Plenty of dust in summer, dirt in winter,
>   And where a woman sitting at her blind
>   Sees all that passes.

Clara responds with a long discourse on the potential
dangers of high-spiritedness, and the importance of un-
blemished reputation—

> EUGENIA. Come, Clara, if the sermon's done,
>   Pray finish it officially at once,
>   And let us out of church. These homilies
>   In favour of defunct proprieties,
>   Remind me of old ruff and armour worn
>   By Don Punctilio and Lady Etiquette
>   A hundred years ago, and passed with them
>   And all their tedious ancestors for ever.
>   I am alive, young, handsome, witty, rich,
>   And come to town, and mean to have my fling,
>   Not caring what malicious people say,
>   If nothing true to say against my honour.

It would be worth reading Calderon if it were only to be
reminded that ' the modern girl ', so far from being a
specifically English or American twentieth-century product,
was familiar in Spain three hundred years ago. Unfortu-
nately, the dramatist gives little scope to Eugenia, and
Clara's ' still waters ' are all too shallow. *Beware of Smooth
Water* is a play of lost opportunities, both on account of

the two sisters and also of the cousin who comes to marry one of them. This Don Torribio Cuadradillos promises at first to be as good as Tony Lumpkin and Mr. Collins put together, but Calderon does not succeed in making him more than a plain ordinary ass with one exceedingly bright moment when he mistakes a farthingale (whalebone petticoat frame) for a collapsible ladder. There is no special discredit to Calderon in saying (it has to be said about most dramatists) that he could begin a play much better than he could end one. It is, however, a less common weakness that he could ' state ' his characters well but could not develop them, nor even sustain them. This is obvious in his comic characters, who often start amusingly, but usually have only one funny trick in their repertory. Thus Leonelo in *The Painter of Dishonour* has an entertaining habit of illustrating his conversation with anecdotes—one about ' a certain man in Barcelona who had five or six children ' which he never succeeds in telling—but he fades out after the first act.

The extent to which we take account of Calderon's limitations is at least a measure of the interest he arouses in us. He had no such fundamental grasp of human nature as Molière had, while he also lacked Molière's intellectual passion and moral seriousness. Yet he survives on account of some inherent quality that is independent of his significance as a landmark in Spanish literature, and for stage purposes he is certainly not finally out-moded.

CHAPTER VI

GERMANY

§ 1—*Ground Plan*

THOUGH German literature is as voluminous as any and its influence far-reaching, its significance does not arise from a long succession of 'great' figures, but rather from the unique intimacy of association between the German people and their literature, their poetry particularly. Most nations possess a body of folk poetry and folk story, but the tendency, as civilization enfeebles primitive instincts and impulses, is for men and women to grow away from what may be termed home-made literature and to rely more and more upon what is supplied by professional writers. Consequently, in England and elsewhere in recent times, interest in folk poetry (the ballads) and folk song and dance has become an artificially stimulated cult—a pious educational crusade more than a spontaneous affection for old things and old ways. In Germany, however, local attachment to the popular poetry and national legends has never been altogether severed, while much even of the later cultured poetry is embedded in the general memory through the German devotion to group singing. Thus, both the old poetry and the newer, as well as the epic legends of the Nibelungs, have played a larger part in the emotional and mental experience of the Germans than anything in English literature has contributed to our own national make-up. Hardly until the end of the eighteenth century can German literature be said to have become a 'wonder of the world', and it is only with considerable pains that foreigners, groping amid a host of unfamiliar works, can follow the main line of development. Once again the language question is important, and the sixteenth century was well on its way before a sufficiently command-ing personality arose to set a firm foundation that would give one dialect an assured preference over others. The fact must be borne in mind that the unification of the numerous German principalities and ducal states was not achieved until a much later date. There was consequently no *a priori* reason why the language of any one State more than another should become Germany's ' national ' language. But Luther (1483–1546) found the Saxon tongue in fairly general use for official purposes, and, employing it for his translation of the Bible (1522 ; 1534), made Middle German the national literary language.

Before Luther, the outstanding production among a considerable mass of epic narratives spread over several hundred years was the *Nibelungenlied* which, by the begin-ning of the thirteenth century, had taken the form in which we know it. By that date the original combination of pagan myth, hero saga and historical incident had received a substantial veneer of Christian conviction, but the veneer is transparent and the essential paganism remains. The King Arthur cycle also penetrated into Germany, where it was worked upon both by imitators and transformers, and reached its noblest manifestation in the *Parzival* of Wol-.fram von Eschenbach (*c.* 1170–*c.* 1220). But the greatest single figure in German medieval literature was Walther von der Vogelweide (*c.* 1168–*c.* 1228), alternately a Court poet and a wandering singer, equally accomplished as a maker of love lyrics and religious and patriotic poems. The period in which Walther flourished was the great age of *Minnelieder* (idealized love songs with a close affinity to the Provençal troubadour lays).

German drama in its early stages passed through a course of development closely analogous to that in England, but the interest of German artisans ran strongly in another

channel also. The trade guilds in many large towns
formed flourishing singing clubs which grew from small
beginnings to elaborately organized affairs culminating in
the great *Meistersinger* festivals familiar to the world
through Wagner's opera. Side by side with these singing
clubs, and probably at first (until complexity drew them
apart) in conjunction with them, there was a great outpouring of popular poetry by anonymous authors.

One of the earliest German books to secure a wide public
outside its native country was *The Ship of Fools*, in which
the author, Sebastian Brant (1457–1521), plays more than
a hundred variations upon the subject of human folly, with
a satirical touch and a moral intent. But widespread
though the influence of this book was, it was to be eclipsed
by the potency of a very different work, the story of Dr.
Faust. Appearing first in 1587, the Faust-book soon began
its fertilizing career. Marlowe's *Dr. Faustus* came out in
1588, and in the intervening three centuries and more this
parable has never lost its hold upon the human imagination.
Meanwhile a universal jester had been added to the world's
small gallery of that type by the growth before 1500 of the
Till Eulenspiegel legend. Grimmelshausen's *Simplicissimus*
(1669), virtually the first German novel, is an entertaining
compound of *picaresque* fiction and autobiography.

From the seventeenth century onward, Germany absorbed
many foreign books in translation, somewhat to the limitation and injury of native genius. This admiration of
foreign works and ideas was carried to its extreme by
Frederick the Great who, in the mid-eighteenth century,
made his Court a replica of the Versailles of Louis XIV. In
1748, however, the true German genius was vindicated by
the issue of *The Messiah* (Cantos I to III) by Klopstock
(1724–1803). The poem ran to twenty cantos and publication was completed in 1773. While *The Messiah* does not
bear comparison with Milton, by whom Klopstock was in

part inspired, it is nevertheless a great poem with a masterly sweep in its vision of the divine plan, and it also evinces a considerable imaginative ability. The advent of Lessing (1729–1781) brought modern German writers into the foreground of world literature. Best known abroad for his *Laokoon*, a valuable treatise on aesthetics and one of the few classics of criticism, Lessing was also a great as well as a successful dramatist, in comedy (*Minna von Barnhelm*), in domestic tragedy (*Miss Sara Sampson*), and in philosophical poetic drama (*Nathan the Wise*). Another literary critic, Herder (1744–1803), also left his independent mark upon contemporary thought, but is chiefly remembered for his association with Goethe, upon whom he had a considerable influence. Goethe (1749–1832) remains to the present day the supreme German literary genius, even though his earlier period coincided with a wave of romanticism that encouraged a disproportionate emphasis upon individualism and that Byronic self-pity which is Rousseau's introspection run to sentimental excess. This phase of Goethe's mental and emotional progress is seen in *Werther*, produced when he was twenty-five. It was from Herder that he had received the doctrine of romantic enthusiasm and passion for originality, in direct contrast with Lessing's cool intellectualism, but Goethe's later experience exercised a moderating and maturing influence, and his plays *Iphigenie auf Tauris* and *Torquato Tasso* (completed round about his fortieth year) show an access of classical restraint. He worked upon *Faust* for many years before publishing the completed first part in 1808, after which a long interval was to elapse before the much more metaphysical second part appeared (1833). Goethe was far from being a one-book man. His fame rests upon *Faust*, but it could rest equally surely upon his lyrical poetry, and perhaps, alternatively, upon what we now regard as his secondary plays. His novel, *Wilhelm Meister*, belongs to a particular psychological mode which is now out of fashion, though its profusion of incidental matter and neglect of organic form bring it close in style to the present-day plotless novel. The third great genius, Schiller (1759–1805), was equally fertile, perhaps even more catholic in his range, and his mental development was not unlike Goethe's in its transition from early impatience of restraint to a mature mood of serenity. His finest work, *Wallenstein*, a tragedy of gigantic proportions, does not rival the profundity of *Faust*; but since *Faust* in its second part soars beyond the possibilities of stage representation, *Wallenstein* ranks as the greatest play for the theatre in German literature. In Heine (1797–1856) the German lyric recaptured a good deal of its old simplicity of mood and material, but presented with the devices of accomplished poetic art. At his best, Heine's tenderness and songfulness place him high among the lyrical poets of all time.

Only one or two writers later than Heine are more than names outside Germany, and a summary note must suffice for these and others who should be mentioned. Grillparzer (1791–1872) turned from German poetic drama to works based upon Greek myth and legend (of which his dramatic trilogy *The Golden Fleece* is the most remarkable), and thence to themes drawn from recent history. Hebbel (1813–1863), a pioneer of German realism, introduced the problem play; and Spielhagen (1829–1911) used the novel for a corresponding purpose. More recently, Sudermann (b. 1857) and Hauptmann (b. 1862) have carried on the realistic drama with considerable force and effect. But of all German writers during the last half-century Nietzsche (1844–1900) has been most discussed by English-speaking people. His proclamation of the superman, free from conventional restraints and normal limitations, is in line with much modern thought and current political doctrine. During the war Nietzsche's reputation abroad dropped considerably, among those who regarded him as the advocate of German ruthlessness, but his best known book *Thus Spake Zarathustra* is now reclaiming attention.

§ 2—*The Nibelungenlied*

During the nineteenth century a revived interest in myth and legend led several European poets to utilize these old stories in the production of modern works. Classical, Celtic and Teutonic legends were laid under contribution in this way—in England by Keats and Shelley, Tennyson, Swinburne and Morris among others; and in Germany perhaps most importantly by Wagner. Of the later writers among those named, Wagner claims special attention, inasmuch as his *Ring of the Nibelungs* has more force as an original work than is usual with modern adaptations of legendary matter. The *Ring* has greater majesty and strength than the old *Lay of the Nibelungs* upon which it is based, whereas Tennyson's *Idylls of the King* are a tamed and feminized offshoot of the *Morte d'Arthur*. It has to be noted, however, that the Nibelung story has taken a variety of forms, according to whether the greater impress was received from German or from Scandinavian sources; and Wagner drew upon the more dramatic and imaginatively fateful northern version rather than upon the spacious and semi-Christianized *Nibelungenlied* with its closer German relationship. If in a phrase the two main forms can be particularized, it can best be done by referring to the medieval German as a history-legend and to the Scandinavian as a fate-myth. In the story as Wagner treated it, Siegfried is the centre toward which everything is directed and from which it radiates. In the medieval German *Nibelungenlied* Siegfried is killed less than halfway through the sequence of adventures; while Hagen, his assassin, is

the principal figure in the second part and stands as a figure
of almost more heroic stature than Siegfried himself.
Brunhild in the *Lay* is little more than a faint shadow of
Brunnhilde in the *Ring* : in fact it might not be extravagant
to say that, compared with Wagner's great warrior queen,
Brunhild is little more impressive than a circus strong
woman. The trend of the two versions—the medieval and
the Wagnerian—is, of course, toward opposite ways, and
the dominant moods entirely diverse. The *Nibelungenlied*
has quite patently been subjected to strong monastic
influences, however uneasily the references to religious
ritual and Christian observances may sit upon the old
blood and vengeance story. In the *Ring*, on the other
hand, Wagner has retained a wholly pagan atmosphere ;
even if the pagan theocracy totters it is no Christian system
that undermines it. The key-idea of the *Ring* is stated by
Brunnhilde before she leaps upon Siegfried's funeral pyre :

> Though gone like breath
> be the godly race,
> though lordless I leave
> behind me the world :
> my holiest wisdom's wealth
> to the world I now reveal.—
> Not goods nor gold,
> nor glory of gods ;
> not house nor hall,
> nor lordly pomp ;
> nor guileful bargain's
> treacherous bonds,
> nor feigning custom's
> hard decrees—
> *blessing in weal and woe*
> *Love alone can bring !* [1]

Magic, awe and wonder are also much more prominent in
the *Ring* than in the *Lay*. Siegfried in the latter has a
magic cloak (Tarnkappe) wrested by him from Albric the

[1] Jameson's translation.

dwarf, but that is almost the only piece of supernatural machinery employed. There are no Rhinemaidens (though in Part II of the *Lay* there are some unconvincing mermaids with prophetic abilities ; one of them is an aunt and they all wear clothes !) ; Siegfried's sword, Balmung, is given to him, not forged with impressive circumstance as Nothung is in the *Ring*. One happy touch in the medieval story, however, occurs in connection with Siegfried's vulnerable spot. In Wagner, it will be remembered, Brunnhilde neglected to make Siegfried invulnerable in the back, because, as she says, he would never turn his back to a foe. Kriemhild (who in the *Nibelungenlied* corresponds to Gutrune in Wagner's *The Twilight of the Gods*) tells Hagen (then posing as her husband's protector) :

When Siegfried slew the dragon on the mountain he bathed in its blood ; wherefore no weapon can pierce him. . . . And now, dear cousin, I will trust thee with the secret, and tell thee, that thou mayst prove thy faith, where my husband may be wounded. For that I know thee honourable I do this. When the hot blood flowed upon the wound of the dragon, and Siegfried bathed therein, there fell atween his shoulders the broad leaf of a lime tree. There one might stab him, and thence is my care and dole.[1]

The lime-tree leaf is a simple and natural device, more homely and less heroic than that used by Wagner.

What has been said in contrasting the *Lay* with the *Ring* serves to establish two essential differences. First, that the *Nibelungenlied* is a piece of minstrelsy which, like all such, has evidently undergone slow growth with additions and changes that have flattened and loosened whatever harmony of design it may at first have had. *The Ring of the Nibelungs*, on the contrary, as the work of one hand, has both a unified aesthetic pattern and a single ethical design —both of which may be more economically achieved in the dramatic form than in the epic. Secondly, Siegfried is

[1] Margaret Armour's translation.

exalted by Wagner to the stature of a modern national (and something more than national) hero ; therefore every means is used to amplify his impressiveness, and he is, indeed, a magnificent creation—perhaps the only example in modern literature of a truly heroic figure in any way comparable with the traditional heroes. In the medieval *Nibelungenlied*, however, as has been said, the customary dominating epic figure is lacking, because of Siegfried's early disappearance and because of Hagen's unfitness for the rôle of hero.

For the purpose of referring to particular features, a brief summary of the *Lay* may usefully be given. By the Rhine, at Worms in Burgundy, lived Kriemhild, sister to three princes, Gunther, Gernot, and Giselher. Among their knights was Hagen of Tronje. In the north, Siegfried (son of Siegmund and Sieglind) had earned widespread fame for his many exploits, among these being the capture of the Nibelung's treasure which he committed the dwarf Albric to guard in its cave. Siegfried came at length to Worms to woo Kriemhild, whom he married after many labours in the field. Meanwhile Gunther had travelled to Issland, where lived Brunhild, who would accept no suitor unless he could excel her at spear-play and at stone-hurling and leaping. Those who failed in the contest died. By Siegfried's aid in the invisible cloak, Gunther won Brunhild, but she would not suffer his husbandly caresses. At this stage in the *Lay* there are passages of rare humour concerning the manner in which Gunther is treated by his wife, especially when he complains to Siegfried : ' Shame and hurt have I suffered from my wife in my house. When I would have caressed her, she bound me tight, and took me to a nail, and hung me up on the wall. There I dangled in fear the night through till the day, or she loosed me. How soft she lay there ! I tell thee this in secret.' Once again Siegfried subdued her, though Brunhild, in acknowledging defeat, thought it was Gunther who ' gripped her till the joints of her body cracked '. In the darkness Siegfried took Brunhild's ring and girdle and gave them to his wife, Kriemhild, when he told her the story. After some years, during which Siegfried and Kriemhild return to his home in the north, they again visit Gunther's court. Brunhild has grown jealous of Kriemhild, and the two women quarrel over matters of precedence. Producing the ring and girdle, Kriemhild taunts Brunhild with having had Siegfried as her lover. From this quarrel follows the death of Siegfried at Hagen's hand while they are resting by a stream. Up to that point the only definite stated moral is ' Women must be taught to bridle their tongues '. The bare story here outlined is everywhere embroidered in the full narrative by those arts familiar in stories which have passed through the process of oral delivery by court minstrels : details of tournaments, descriptions of embroidered and bejewelled dresses, gatherings of armed men —all the bustle and occupations, the comings and goings, that made up court life in the chivalric age. From the point at which Siegfried is slain, however, the *Nibelungenlied* becomes a tale of revenge and retribution with Kriemhild and Hagen as the chief protagonists. In the early days of her widowhood, the great Nibelung treasure is brought into Worms for Kriemhild, who spends long years in lamentation and good works. Ultimately—after Hagen has caused the bulk of the Nibelung's gold to be taken from her and sunk in the Rhine—she is persuaded to marry the Hun king, Etzel. In the seventh year thereafter, obsessed by a tormenting desire to be avenged on those by whom she had been wronged, Kriemhild asks Etzel to invite her kinsmen to visit them. They come, against Hagen's counsel, and the last twelve or more adventures in the *Lay* are stories of the carnage that was done in the warfare that breaks out between the visitors and their hosts. Throughout this part the two heroes are Hagen and Folker the Fiddler.

Sympathy veers round completely—in favour of Hagen and against Kriemhild, though the latter is by far the most skilfully depicted character among them all. She is the only one in whom any dramatic development can be seen, or who is perceptibly moulded by experience and circumstance. Her love for Siegfried eats into her soul after his murder, and one can observe how her whole nature becomes emptied of all but this. Sorrow and inward desolation grow to a canker. This is assuaged for a time by the new affections and interests her second marriage brings, but eventually the old obsession returns, now aggravated by a consciousness of power. And so she sweeps on a full tide of malignancy to her revenge. Hagen kills Siegfried; Kriemhild kills Hagen; Hildebrand kills Kriemhild; in the end, ' dead bodies lay stretched over all '.

It is possible to see in the early adventures the germ of that primitive nature-myth to which all such stories are traced back by some scholars. Siegfried (if this theory is accepted) is undoubtedly the young Spring God (or the Daystar) who in due season has to die at the hand of his enemy Winter (or Night) personified here by Hagen. But there (so far as the *Lay* in this particular form is concerned) the nature-myth goes underground, and the story becomes a complicated record of bloody revenge. Nevertheless, in one shape or another, the Nibelung legend stimulated the national consciousness of Germany from the mid-nineteenth century onward, and it is in a double degree—in its medieval manifestation and in its modern revival—a landmark in that century's literature.

§ 3—*Goethe : Faust*

The human mind swings pendulum-like between periods when it is content to submit to authority—religious, political, social—and periods when it feels an urgent need to throw over authority, freeing itself from the pressure of discipline and restraint. Even if the imposition of and submission to authority did not in due course breed abuses or encourage tyranny, man would still feel the need to revitalize himself by bathing in the fiery spirit of revolt. Man cannot stagnate—and live. He cannot content himself with contentment. Struggle, within or without, is a law of being, and it could be said that if discontent did not exist it would be necessary to invent it.

We may with some justification feel, therefore, that impatience toward authority is not only primitive and fundamental but also inevitable and essential. Man must grow, and he grows as the shoot from the seed grows, by pushing away that which is over him—apparently restraining and oppressing him, apparently stunting his growth— though like the good earth lying heavily upon the seed it may be a main factor in his growth. As the plant needs not only soil to hold its roots but also light and air and the power to reach these, man requires not only traditions for his basis but also the outward-reaching power to the light and air he feels to be above him, impalpable but very real.

It is not fantastic—far otherwise, it is a commonplace— to suggest that the spirit of revolt (this recurring tendency to kick over the traces) is inherent in man. If it were not so, Lucifer, Prometheus and Faust would have no permanent place in literature and thought. Rather strangely, of these three only Prometheus is generally regarded as a thoroughly 'respectable' rebel—he was, of course, noble, disinterested and endlessly courageous; and yet Shelley, in part a modern Prometheus, was accounted far from respectable; even as Prometheus himself would be if he could emerge from myth and live to-day. It is, however, just worth noting that all three stories—of Lucifer, Prometheus, and Faust—embody the same idea, defiance of authority and the human right to determine individual action and destiny. They are proclamations in extreme form of the principle of free will, of the will to be so completely free that a man may, if he so choose, cast his soul into ever-lasting damnation, for there is this something in us fostering the belief that no price is too high for liberty and the right to rebel.

As is well known, the Faust legend had been floating in the western imagination for centuries before Goethe gave it popular currency. Considering the peculiar temper aroused by the Renaissance it was almost inevitable that some such universal story should come into existence. Such typical Renaissance men as Marlowe embodied strong intellectual and physical lusts—and spiritual lusts, too. They had an unbridled desire for experiment in every direction, and the necessary factors for this were more knowledge, wealth and power ; the quest of these three is the theme of Marlowe's plays. Naturally he took up the Faust story, then well known in western Europe through the German Faust-book.

Those exhausting Renaissance desires subsided as men either grew tired or became habituated to their enlarged universe. But when the spirit of political and intellectual revolt stirred in France during the eighteenth century, corresponding unrest was displayed elsewhere in Europe. England felt it ; so also did Germany, where one phase of this unrest manifested itself in the interest taken by young men in the phenomena of witchcraft and in that monument of witchcraft (or wizardry) the Faust story. If Satan be regarded as the symbol of revolt and witches as the hand-maids of Satan, it is not difficult to detect an associative link between the interest in witchcraft and the revolutionary impulse. Goethe as a young man became infected by this interest and began to work on his own version of *Faust* when he was twenty-four. He laboured at it for over fifty years before the second part was published, and into the great poem he poured his whole power. The result as we have it is a combination of philosophy and spiritual profundity with fine poetry, rich human interest and emotional simplicity.

Marlowe's *Dr. Faustus* fails (except for its occasional great poetry) because the dramatist does not give the young scholar desires of a magnitude proportionate to the bargain he has made with Mephistopheles. Having bartered his soul he asks for very little more than a series of second-rate magician's tricks. It is not quite certain that Goethe's Faust has an adequate conception of value for value in the bargain, but at least Goethe himself makes the play (with its prolonged philosophical footnote, the second part) carry an impressive weight of intellectual and spiritual significance.

Following (in the Prelude upon the Stage) a full discussion of the dramatist's problem as he faces his material, the Prologue in Heaven surveys man's state in the world and his future progress as seen by Satan and God. 'Mephistopheles' complete pessimism is lightened by shrewdness and some humour—as when he suggests that God long ago forgot how to laugh. His diagnosis of the Faust temperament accurately distinguishes the burning unrest, monstrous ambition and ingrained melancholy that mark the type, though it is God who utters the true apologia for man the rebel by acknowledging that so long as he strives so long must the danger of misdirection be incurred. This prologue, with its colloquially easy dialogue between the two Personages, was for some time regarded as blasphemous by Goethe's critics, but its value as an integral part of the theme requires no demonstration. In the first scene, Faust, discovered in his chamber, is represented as worn out by a sense of the impotence of science, wherefore he turns to magic. But finding no comfort in that, he breaks into a prolonged lamentation over the pains of human life.

He feels the burden of the soul's confinement in mortality, and expresses the sensation that must have been Goethe's own (since it is shared by every genius) of knowing himself at once ' so small ' and yet ' so great '. There, in a single line, Goethe penetrated to the heart of human mystery, though without illuminating what must always remain mysterious. Man is a rebel for a reason lying altogether outside his hatred of oppression. He is a rebel because, made in the likeness of God, he has godlike potentialities always at war with the confining body. Man is a dynamo in a matchbox. If the dynamo—man's full spiritual energy —were released to run at full load, the matchbox which is the body would splinter and burst asunder. Man's spirit and intellect have consequently to be curtailed to the match-box standard, except in those few experiences of ecstasy that are possible in a lifetime—for some, through a mystical religious illumination ; for others, through physical love in its very rare moments of perfect communion. That man should be at once so great and so small is the root of the human tragedy.

Faust agrees to pledge his soul to Mephistopheles in exchange for happiness, since he has found the pursuit of knowledge purposeless, and he plunges into dissipation and debauchery culminating in the bestiality of the witches' kitchen and the Walpurgis Night. Contrasting with this are the scenes where Margaret appears, and the beauty of the love episodes. This thread of loveliness is probably remembered by most people more than anything else in *Faust*, though the sinister insinuating genius of Mephis-topheles is Goethe's truly great dramatic triumph. The one moment at which Marlowe is superior to Goethe purely as a dramatist (he is never Goethe's inferior as a poet) is at the end of *Dr. Faustus*. Faustus' last agonizing cry is one of the overwhelming moments in world literature—a sudden distillation of pure genius. Goethe's ending (to Part I), with its cry of divine redemption for Margaret, is no doubt spiritually more majestic, though it is less effective as drama.

The second part of *Faust* has no essential relation to what goes before. It is in all intents and purposes an independent work. Whether it is greater or less great can only be settled according to the reader's individual preference for drama or philosophy. Goethe was an old man when he wrote the later part, and at that time his bent was much more mystical than literary, and the general judgment would almost certainly be found to agree with G. H. Lewes' verdict that the second part fails because it is not an interesting story with a secondary symbolical meaning, but is a sequence of symbols having no continuous interest and requiring a key before it can be comprehended. Probably it has been in general no better understood than Blake's prophetic books. The multitudes of characters and the diffusion of meaning place it beyond the resources of theatrical production, and the most profitable way to approach it is as a miscellany in which a good deal of beautiful poetry and some illuminating thought is to be found. We shall not then be teased by an unavailing expectation of continuity and coherence. Faust himself, in Part II, can be said either to have achieved peace and wisdom, or to have become a spiritual renegade—again it depends upon the judge's point of view. To a character named Care, Faust discourses upon the vanity and illusiveness of human desires and majestic passions, and advises contentment with what the little world offers. This tired-old-man's counsel misses its mark because it suggests no solution for the problem of the dynamo in the matchbox.

CHAPTER VII

RUSSIA

§ 1—*Ground Plan*

STANDING midway between East and West, Russia is both a barrier and a link. Its literature has the intellectual penetration of European culture within an amorphous outline that is the product of an oriental tendency toward a way of life which seems to the western mind unpurposive and misty rather than mystical; a kind of breathing upon life's window-pane instead of a practical facing of what we call ' life's problems '. The difference between those who are naturally drawn toward the exterior life of action and those who concentrate upon the interior life of spiritualized contemplation and imaginative speculation is fundamental, but not uninterchangeable. The west has been influenced in recent decades by Russian literature more than by any other and has absorbed some of its main characteristics; while, under Soviet rule, Russia has become infected by the feverous practical activity of mechanistic western civilization. The effects of this interchange will provide problems for the next generation to unravel.

English readers are poorly equipped to appreciate Russian literature, for the supply of adequate translations has been spasmodic, and outside the half-dozen leading writers whose works have been more or less completely translated there are ludicrous gaps, and equally ludicrous fillings where minor and second-rate books have been translated while much of Pushkin and Lermontov and (among more recent writers) Remizov and others is still neglected. Add to this the lack of uniformity in the English transliteration of

Russian names, as well as the absence of standard translations of many book-titles, and it will be seen that much work has still to be done before English readers can judge Russian literature without grotesque misconceptions of its general character.

To begin even the briefest sketch of Russian literary history at 1820 may seem fantastic, but actually there had been little of supreme importance before that date. The early centuries, from roughly 1100 onward, produced quantities of religious writing in prose and verse, but up to the late seventeenth century there are hardly more than two really notable secular works : the prose poem, *Prince Igor* (*c.* 1200), belonging to the period when Kiev was still an important centre, before the Tartars overran Russia (*c.* 1200–1250) ; and an autobiography, *The Life of the Archpriest Avvakum*, the author of which was burned at the stake in 1681 in consequence of his opposition to certain modifications in church practice introduced by the then ruling Patriarch. Avvakum was thus martyred in upholding the convictions of the ' old believers ', who maintained their corporate identity for many generations and have a place in later novels.

The accession of Peter the Great gave an impetus to intellectual and cultural activity in St. Petersburg shortly after 1700, and the resultant literary stirring preluded the great achievements to come in the next age. Pushkin (1799–1837) is the greatest of all Russian poets, and since his greatness is of the universal order he has comparatively little of the characteristic and peculiar ' Russianness ' that belongs to many of his successors. His genius was shaped by familiarity with French and English writers, but though the romanticism of Byron influenced him much it was nevertheless controlled by a classical sense of order. This ' normality ' (as it might be called) in Pushkin makes him unremarkable to foreign readers ; but since it was allied with a power of giving heroic stature to Russian themes, it provides just that stability and balance which makes him for Russians the great classic national poet. Selecting from much that was good, the narrative poem *Eugene Onegin*, the dramatic epic-chronicle *Boris Godunov*, and the novel *The Captain's Daughter*, may be named as among Pushkin's masterpieces. Lermontov (1814–1841), known abroad for his remarkable analytical novel *A Hero of our Time*—the first of its kind in Russia—was also a great poet, but it is rather with Gogol (1809–1852) that Russian literature first becomes directly known in the West. His satirical comedy *The Inspector-General* is an attack on corrupt and inept officialdom, but it is also an affair of hearty laughter. Gogol had a particular aptitude for the kind of caricature which is both larger and truer than life because it strips away the covering veils that hide men's true selves from the sight of their fellows. The technical devices used in *The Inspector-General* sometimes seem clumsy in comparison with our later and neater stagecraft—especially the frequent use of asides—and the action is inclined to be flat and unduly obvious. But the play is none the less a great comic achievement and would deserve a place in any world repertory.[1] Gogol's novel, *Dead Souls*, rings with a much more bitter laughter than is heard in *The Inspector-General*. Yet merciless as is the laying bare of Chichikov's despicable character in *Dead Souls*, Gogol's final attitude toward this universal rogue is one of deep understanding and comprehensive pity which tempers judgment with almost as liberal a measure of mercy as may be found unceasingly in Chekhov. No better picture has been provided of Russian provincial life than in three volumes of memories by Aksakov (1791–1859) —*Years of Childhood*, *A Russian Schoolboy*, and *A Russian Gentleman*—sane, exact, and rich in likeable and skilfully depicted people.

[1] The greatest Russian comedy, *The Misfortune of Being Clever*, by Griboyedov (1795–1829) is still unknown in England.

With Turgenev (1816–1883), Dostoevsky (1818–1881), and Tolstoy (1828–1910) we reach the three writers who made Russia a preponderating influence upon the intellectual outlook of the western world. But no proper understanding of Turgenev's and Dostoevsky's place in nineteenth-century Russian literature is to be had without considering them in relation to the revolutionary fervour of the time. Not that either of them can be accounted in any sense a practical revolutionary, but they became symbols of political and social enlightenment, and both suffered exile, Dostoevsky actually being sentenced to death with others in 1849 and reprieved at the foot of the gallows. Tolstoy's immunity from political persecution was due to the inability of the dullest official mind to overlook the danger of attempting to overturn a colossus. Turgenev's work has more marks of pictorial artistry about it than the others', though he is not so great a literary artist as they. But with Turgenev the peasant comes imperishably into Russian literature, and with him begins, too, that humanitarian cult of the under-dog which has since run like an epidemic through English as well as Russian writings. The impressionistic nature of his work—both descriptively and emotionally—makes him a literary Corot. No one else has ever carried metaphysical dissection so far as it is carried in Dostoevsky's *Crime and Punishment* and *The Brothers Karamazov*. These two novels represent the ultimate achievement in that kind of writing : they seem to be the product of a more than human genius—the product, as it were, of a divine anatomist who is also a superb artist. Tolstoy can only be ranked above Dostoevsky by those who agree to compare the incomparable. Men and women appear to grow, granule by granule, in Tolstoy's novels till we have at length complete persons and even complete communities of persons. But in Dostoevsky's it is the process of disintegration that we watch, the division of human personality granule from granule. The former process is more gratifying than the latter, but also less magnificently terrifying. For two or three generations past, Tolstoy has been lauded as a major prophet by foreigners, possibly beyond his due. He had no valid message that was not already present in the New Testament ; and as a prophet he must be finally ineffective because his asceticism was too suspiciously like the diseased product of an exhausted sensualist terrified by the lure of indulgences he had enjoyed freely aforetime. But no charge of distemper and perversity of outlook and argument can make him less than marvellous as a creator, a recreator, of people and scenes which have all the detailed richness and almost more than the truth and conviction of life itself. If the sustained illusion of actuality inspired by the spirit of living truth is the highest product of art, then Tolstoy is the supreme literary artist and *War and Peace* the world's foremost novel.

To come in the wake of a triad of giants is a crippling disability, and the stature of more recent Russian writers is somewhat diminished by proximity to Tolstoy and Dostoevsky. Ostrovsky (1823–1886) wrote interesting naturalistic plays ; *Who Can be Happy and Free in Russia ?* by Nekrassov (1821–1877) is an example of humanitarian naturalism in verse ; Maxim Gorky (*b.* 1869) began with realistic stories of underworld life, and afterwards displayed genius of a new order in his autobiographical records ; Andreyev (1871–1919), one of the strongest among the contemporary writers, relied in his plays and stories more than enough upon the violent contrast of red and black ; and Sologub (*b.* 1863), Remizov (*b.* 1877), Biely (*b.* 1880), and Blok (1880–1921) are but a few among a multitude whose work will no doubt be better known abroad in the future. The one acknowledged master since the great period is Chekhov (1860–1904), whose short stories and plays have been acclaimed in England far more than in Russia, where he represents the last throes of a decaying civilization. By us, however, Chekhov is valued for his painfully smiling and inexhaustible charity of temper, born of unlimited love and perfect understanding. For him men and women were men and women, all of them in a particular situation, and in that situation worthy of attention independent of whether the people or the situation happened to be 'important'. His art is subtle beyond analysis and the play of humour over his work is like the moving pattern of sunlight falling through light clouds upon a wind-ruffled field.

§ 2—*Tolstoy* : *War and Peace*

There was published in London not long after the war began in 1914 a pamphlet under some such title as *The World's Debt to Russia*. Its coloured pictorial cover suggested to the ordinary English mind a castle in Spain rather than anything Russian, but the point to note is that the British propagandist originators of the pamphlet had then no doubt that in a variety of ways western civilization was indebted to Russia. Now the situation has changed it still remains true that we are thus indebted, though it is found expedient not to recall the facts too precisely. Any fair attempt to assess the extent of the debt would have to take account of Russia's influence for at least half a century on western music, decorative art, costume, drama, fiction, philosophy and possibly statecraft. Most English people formerly linked Russia with the idea of a prevalent drabness, as they do now with a predominant redness, but in the supposedly drab nineteenth-century period it was colour as much as anything that Russia contributed to European culture. When thinking of Russian people we are far too prone to take a flat generalized impression of a nation which is almost infinitely diversified; which stretches over a vast tract of the earth's surface with climatic differences ranging between the arctic and the sub-tropical; and which has racial characteristics in some respects more closely allied with eastern tendencies than with western. So far as any distinctively Russian personal make-up can be isolated from a mass of differences, it would be true to say that the Russian mind is more fluid than, for example, the English mind. It is consequently much more sensitive as a recording instrument, and much more elusive in its movements. The fundamental unlikeness of the two types of mind and soul can be detected by English readers of Tolstoy's *Childhood, Boyhood and Youth*, with its account of (to us) trivial happenings that seemed (and in effect were) catastrophic to the Russian boy. To attempt to dismiss these differences by declaring that they arise from a morbidly introspective habit, is as foolish as if we were to accuse a seismograph of morbid introspection because it records earth tremors unfelt by us. From that acute sensitiveness arises, in the great Russian nineteenth-century novelists, the peculiar quality of apparently overstressed sympathy with all despitefully-used creatures, with all who seem in one way or another to be victimized—the poor, the broken, the outcast, the depressed, the unsuccessful. Tolstoy was, on the whole, more robust in this respect than some of his contemporaries; though there was that in Tolstoy which caused him to interpret the Sermon on the Mount much more literally than we feel is practicable. And it was this same tendency, also, which gave him his amazing analytical power and the ability to create 'the illusion of absolute truth', his most remarkable and unsurpassed gift.

From the first, Tolstoy displayed a didactic outlook. Though an anti-romantic in some respects, he followed Rousseau in urging the need for man to get back into close touch and harmony with Nature in the attempt to restore man's original excellence before civilization had maimed and degraded him. This was more than mere humanitarian theorizing in Tolstoy. It derived quite as much from his early contacts with untutored primitive types in the Caucasus region (he saw service there with the Russian army), where he came to believe that ' simplicity is the first condition of moral beauty '. *War and Peace* records in detail the experiences of two Russian families, the Bolonskys and the Rostovs, during the fifteen years from 1805. Several characters in the book are modified re-creations of people Tolstoy knew, and the place called Bald Hills is reminiscent of his own estate at Yasnaya Polyana ; but he did not merely copy. Enormously long and detailed, *War and Peace* is less a connected fictional or semi-fictional narrative than a huge chunk of life transplanted to a book. Yet to say that is perhaps to underrate Tolstoy's great merit as a literary artist—probably the finest Russia has had. He sought in this book for absolute realism—realism as it should properly be understood—*all* reality, not only its dark side. Tolstoy's name is associated in many minds with a body of Tolstoyan theories ; but, in earlier years at least, he reversed the usual processes of theorists. He did not attempt to impose set theories upon life, or endeavour to mould experience in conformity with preconceived notions. He held that life itself is the great teacher, and that it is sounder to trust ' the subconscious wisdom of the race ' than acquired knowledge and culture. Therefore, in *War and Peace*, he makes Karataev the peasant soldier a symbolic figure—' an unfathomable, rounded, eternal personification of the spirit of simplicity and truth '.[1]

When *War and Peace* was completed, Tolstoy was forty-one, and he had not yet experienced the conversion which turned him from a literary artist with a strong sense of

---

[1] *War and Peace :* Book XII, Ch. XIII ; Aylmer Maude's translation.

purpose into a religious recluse who yet retained his creative powers. Being a more natural master of the novelist's art than either Dostoevsky or Turgenev, Tolstoy shows a less evident concern with it than they. If his work as a novelist is sometimes imperfect, technically, it is the imperfection of a master who has outgrown the spirit of conformity. And as ' a novelist with a purpose ' Tolstoy is less overcome by life's agony than Dostoevsky was : he contemplates human suffering with more serenity. His sympathies are not exclusively engaged by either aristocracy or peasantry *as a class* ; he is big enough to see that a suffering creature suffers independently of his social status. Although much of *War and Peace* is necessarily concerned with tumult—the external tumult of war and the inward tumult of emotional stresses—the novel as a piece of literature moves in an atmosphere of calm : it considers human problems, as it were, in the light of the whole ; its spiritual perspective is unconfined, and its judgments of human destiny are not solely conditioned by the events of fifteen years' terrestrial conflict. Tolstoy could not ' lose his head ' over human ills, because he took exceptionally long views :

Pierre had learned not with his mind but with his whole being, through life itself, that man is created for happiness, that happiness lies within him, in the natural satisfaction of human needs, and that all unhappiness arises not from privation but from superfluity. . . . He had learned yet another new, consolatory truth—he had learned that there is nothing terrible in the world. He had learned that as there is no condition in which man is happy and entirely free, so there is no condition in which he need be unhappy and not free.[1]

The acknowledged greatness of *War and Peace* arises in part from Tolstoy's power to suggest the immensity outside his book. However extensive and populous the narrative itself may be, we are continuously aware that beyond his

[1] Book XIV, Ch. XII.

presented fragment of a world there is the whole world ; that beyond those fifteen years with their slow changes there is Time ; and beyond Time, Eternity. No other novel surveys the landscape of life with such extraordinary fidelity and truth. It is a landscape in which level downland occupies most space, diversified by occasional hills and backed by a vast mountain range. The mountain range is the Napoleonic campaign ; the hills, the inner crises of the chief characters ; the wide stretches of downland, the daily domestic experiences in the Rostov and Bolonsky families. If any readers find *War and Peace* tedious, it is because they have grown accustomed to the less patient and less true methods used by other nove- lists who ignore the flat interspaces of average experience. Tolstoy does, above all, suggest the *texture* of a daily life that goes on and goes on ; and which yet, while merely going on, is threaded by queer emotional strands. Those who feel that *War and Peace* is longer than it need be are discouraged by this going-on-ness, which makes it the most lifelike book in all literature. The central theme of *War and Peace* is the endless replacement of one generation by the next. As it begins, the younger generation is pressing out the older ; when it closes, that younger generation is within sight of being superseded by the still younger. Time is the tragic hero. The novel's chief technical fault is that it is two novels in one, and the two are imperfectly knitted together. Tacked on to the theme of youth and age is the voluminous account of Napoleon's Russian campaign. This part of the book is an artistic success when Tolstoy forgets that he is Tolstoy and merges himself in Prince Andrew, or Nicholas, or Pierre, letting us see and feel the war through their personalities ; but it is a failure when Tolstoy remains just Tolstoy, lecturing on history and military tactics : then the illusion is broken and for the time being the novel falls into the background. Again and again Tolstoy lets himself be carried away by the conviction (possibly a sound one)

that the supposed 'plans' of military leaders are a combination of muddle and accident. This conviction might
legitimately be stated in a novel, but only on condition that
it is stated *through* the action and characters, and not by the
method of direct address from author to reader. Sometimes, indeed, Tolstoy does succeed in harmonizing the
expression of his anti-war views with the requirements of
the narrative. But, for the most part, considering that the
novel starts out to be (notwithstanding its title) a presentation of individual and family life, the war should have been
utilized as an episode, however immense, in the still larger
experience.

What, finally, is the secret that has given *War and Peace*
so extraordinary a hold upon the admiration, even upon the
affections, of multitudes of readers ? It is to be found in
Tolstoy's genius for creating the illusion of reality so strongly
that all sense of illusion passes away and reality only seems to
remain. These people rise beyond Russianness into univer-
sality. They think, feel, behave, with complete naturalness ;
and as we read we see them growing older page by page as
each fragment of the fifteen years slips away.

§ 3—*Dostoevsky : The Brothers Karamazov*

Tolstoy was, first and foremost, a novelist. He was also
a saint, whose saintliness was injured by too much asceticism.
But he was not a great or original thinker, though England
and America chose at first to idolize him almost purely on
account of his ideas—or, rather, his preachings. He saw
many things very clearly when he looked at them through
the perspective-glass of the New Testament ; when,
however, he looked with his own unaided sight at
some of life's major problems his outlook became much
less sane. He will therefore seem, more and more as time

elapses, to belong to literature and scarcely at all to philosophy.

That needs to be said, not as a footnote to Tolstoy, but as a prelude to Dostoevsky. Anyone who comments upon Dostoevsky must first attempt to decide whether he is to be approached as a novelist—or what ? The question is important, because if he is primarily a novelist, *The Brothers Karamazov*, for example, contains a good deal of superfluous matter which on aesthetic grounds must be regarded as so much ' dead wood '. Certainly we can say with confidence that scores of pages could be cut clean away without injury to the book *as a novel*. It would be a better novel if that were done, yet in becoming a better novel it would cease to be a world-masterpiece. The colossal genius displayed in *The Brothers Karamazov* is a metaphysical genius working with thorough competence in a particular literary medium. The ' dead wood ' to be cut away if a novel and a novel only were required, would include all Ivan's speculations and spiritual probings in Book V, and most of Father Zossima's recollections, conversations and exhortations in Book VI. And if those excisions should be made, the effect would be roughly similar to that which would be produced if an edition of the Bible were produced with only ' the stories ' left in. Unlike Tolstoy, Dostoevsky *was* a profound thinker —though ' thinker ' is possibly too rigid a word to represent Dostoevsky's processes of mystical perception. Only paramount geniuses can be exempted from conformity to literary tradition, otherwise a new literary ' form ' would have to be admitted for every petty caprice pretending to genius. Dostoevsky was a paramount genius : a spiritual and intellectual giant who happened incidentally to be a remarkably good novelist in the intervals of his preoccupation with more urgent matters. Readers who have a natural taste for metaphysics will not need any persuasion to read Dostoevsky. But are readers devoid of that taste to think that he is not for them? It would be a pity if they were to think so. Putting for a moment the metaphysics of *The Brothers Karamazov* on one side, there remains (*a*) a first-class ' novel of passion ' and (*b*) a first-class ' thriller '. Dostoevsky's admirers would consider it deplorable that he should be read for either of these attractions ; but since no person of average intelligence could read *The Brothers Karamazov* or any part of it without picking up ideas as involuntarily as burrs are gathered by a skirt, it is better to read it for a trumpery motive than not to read it at all. The second half of the book (that is to say about four hundred pages) contain one of the most skilfully contrived and exciting ' crime stories ' ever written. And much of the first half is devoted to a ruthlessly penetrating analysis of Fyodor Karamazov and his sons Dmitri, Ivan and Alyosha, all three sharing in some measure and in divergent forms the sensualism of the father, in whom it runs to complete animalism. Dmitri ' wallows in dirt and drink ', but is at the same time capable of watching with horror his own degradation, referring to himself in a line of verse as an insect enslaved by sensual lust. When the father is found robbed and murdered, Dmitri is tried for the crime and convicted, the account of the police examination and trial being given by Dostoevsky in extensive and fascinating detail.

The brothers are typically Dostoevskian in their relentless determination to diagnose the nature of what we should call colloquially ' the family failing ', but which is nearer to being the family curse. Dmitri declares, ' I'm a Karamazov. For when I do leap into the pit, I go headlong with my heels up, and am pleased to be falling in that degraded attitude, and pride myself on it.' Alyosha says, ' My brothers are destroying themselves. . . . It's " the primitive force of the Karamazovs ". . . . I, too, am a Karamazov.' And Ivan speaks of the Karamazovs' ' thirst for life regardless of everything '. The father and the three sons are all full and active living men, not abstractions ; some one phase of the family urge is dominant in each : in Fyodor it has run to insatiable lust ; in Dmitri, lust is modified by self-critical detachment ; in Ivan the thirst for life runs in an intellectual and speculative channel ; while in Alyosha it is tempered by a spiritualized and excessive fastidiousness. In a previous section of this chapter, reference has been made to the Russian mind and soul as supersensitive recording instruments. What was meant can be illustrated within a little by quotation from words used by Dmitri, in conversation with Alyosha :

Imagine : inside, in the nerves, in the head—that is, these nerves are there in the brain . . . (damn them !) there are sort of little tails, the little tails of those nerves, and as soon as they begin quivering . . . that is, you see, I look at something with my eyes and then they begin quivering, those little tails . . . and when they quiver, then an image appears . . . it doesn't appear at once, but an instant, a second, passes . . . and then something like a moment appears ; that is, not a moment—devil take the moment !—but an image ; that is an object, or an action, damn it ! That's why I see and then think, because of those tails, not at all because I've got a soul, and that I am some sort of image and likeness.[1]

Such visualization of the processes behind consciousness could scarcely arise anywhere else than in Russian literature ; though, of course, elsewhere in Dostoevsky and others mental and spiritual hypersensitiveness is not necessarily accompanied by interest in the apparatus at work. The meticulous examination of personal responses and motives for action is part and parcel of this sensitiveness, which is shared by Dostoevsky's women in common with the men. A society lady in *The Brothers Karamazov*, having expressed her desire to become a sister of mercy, begins to doubt her ability to

---

[1] Book XI, Ch. IV ; Constance Garnett's translation. The dots in this passage are in the original and do not denote omissions from the quotation.

tolerate the duties that would be imposed upon her, and she cites as applicable to her own feelings certain observations that had been made to her by a doctor :

'I love humanity,' he said, 'but I wonder at myself. The more I love humanity in general, the less I love man in particular. In my dreams,' he said, 'I have often come to making enthusiastic schemes for the service of humanity, and perhaps I might actually have faced crucifixion if it had been suddenly necessary ; and yet I am incapable of living in the same room with anyone for two days together, as I know by experience. As soon as anyone is near me, his personality disturbs my self-complacency and restricts my freedom. In twenty-four hours I begin to hate the best of men : one because he's too long over his dinner; another because he has a cold and keeps on blowing his nose. I become hostile to people the moment they come close to me. But it has always happened that the more I detest men individually the more ardent becomes my love for humanity.'

Dostoevsky's metaphysic, or philosophy, or religious belief (for his faith comprises elements of all these) in this book is too extensive and complex to be condensed into a few sentences. He appears to use several of the characters as his mouthpieces at different times and the apposite extracts would constitute a lengthy testament, not merely a compact creed. Father Zossima states a gospel of universal love ; Father Païssy points out that destructive scientific analysis of the Christian faith, in distinguishing the parts, has blindly overlooked the whole ; and in Alyosha's notes for a Life of Zossima there is a mass of relevant matter, as well as much that is affecting in the early experiences of the future priest. Among Zossima's exhortations are many sayings identical with Dostoevsky's own doctrines. For example (in an enlargement of the gospel of love previously mentioned) :

Love a man even in his sin, for that is the semblance of Divine Love and is the highest love on earth. Love all God's creation, the whole and every grain of sand in it. Love every leaf, every ray of God's light. Love the animals, love the plants, love everything. If you

love everything, you will perceive the divine mystery in things. . . .
Love the animals; God has given them the rudiments of thought
and joy untroubled. . . . Love children especially, for they are sinless
like the angels; they live to soften and purify our hearts and as it
were to guide us.

Such love and longing for life Ivan Karamazov has, too, and
it is he who enjoins that we should ' love life more than the
meaning of it '.

It is becoming an article of faith among students of
Dostoevsky's work that the quintessence of his metaphysic
is in Book V of *The Brothers Karamazov*, in the chapter
called *The Grand Inquisitor*. Ivan had projected a poem to
bear that title, and though it had never been written he
gives Alyosha a full account of what was to be its content
and purport. The setting was to be Seville in the sixteenth
century. One day after the burning of nearly a hundred
heretics by the Inquisition, a Presence appears in the streets
healing and raising from the dead. The Grand Inquisitor
orders His arrest, and visiting the prison tells Him He must
be put to death because, by coming back, He will disturb
the people's hearts and hinder the work committed to the
Church with the Pope as the sole interpreter of the faith.
The Inquisitor implies that the Roman Church by sub-
jugating man's will to itself has conferred true happiness
upon men, since freedom leads to rebellion and rebellion
to misery, whereas conformity leads to happiness. The
Prisoner by intervening between believers and the Church
will destroy the spirit of submission and re-create the spirit
of revolt. In a long and torrentially passionate speech the
Inquisitor declares human happiness to be the sole good, and
records his Church's determination to confer happiness
upon its followers by anysoever means, even though it take
Satan as its guide and know that man will find beyond the
grave nothing but death. The condition for man's happiness is that he should be given earthly bread, that the terrible

burden of free choice should be lifted from his shoulders, that he should have someone to worship and someone to keep his conscience. 'There are three powers, three powers alone, able to conquer and to hold captive for ever the conscience of these impotent rebels for their happiness—those forces are miracle, mystery and authority.' How far Dostoevsky's own convictions followed the line of the Inquisitor's argument will be differently determined by individual readers. Here it is enough to say that the Inquisitor's proclamation raises prose to the level of great poetry; and while one reads, carried along as on a stream of subterranean fire, there is reason to ask whether at such moments as these Dostoevsky did not show himself to be the prince of geniuses.

CHAPTER VIII

SCANDINAVIA

§ 1—*Ground Plan*

LESS is known by English readers concerning the history of Scandinavian literature than about any other, and until the close of the nineteenth century the northern writers had had little effect on our own. The Norse legends had, of course, been disseminated more or less generally over Europe for many generations, and Anglo-Saxon poetry retained perceptible traces of the remote Icelandic ancestry it shares in common with the *Nibelungenlied* and such other Scandinavian hero-myths as the *Eddas*. But these legends belong ultimately to a common stock, and can scarcely be claimed specifically for any one of the three countries—Norway, Denmark, and Sweden—known collectively as Scandinavia.

For several hundred years Norwegian literature was practically inseparable from Danish, for the long political connection between the two countries was accompanied by the cultural predominance of Denmark. The union which began in 1380 lasted until 1814, with Danish as the official language in Norway until round about 1700. .From roughly 1550 there were a few Norwegian poets, chiefly religious, but not until Ludvig Holberg (1684–1754) was there any writer possessing unquestionable genius. Holberg, though born in Norway, was wholly abroad during his last fifty years, travelling extensively and imbibing a good deal of the English spirit while he lived for a period at Oxford. With his work, modern Norwegian and Danish literature begins. He helped to bring his country into touch with the general stream of European culture, and is one of the earliest

writers in whom the typical Norwegian gift for unflinchingly
realistic thought can be seen in operation. Copenhagen,
however, remained the literary centre, with Christiania out
of the picture, though a growing spirit of national pride led a
group of poets living in Copenhagen to found the Norwegian
Society in 1772—with Johan Wessel (1742–1785), Johan
Brun (1745–1816), and Claus Frimann (1746–1829) as its
principal members. Wessel's humorous narratives in verse,
distinguished by a genuine creative gift and a genial, lively
and free spirit, are among the best things of their kind in
Norwegian literature. In the second decade of the nineteenth century a literary reawakening began ; and a little
later, Henrik Wergeland (1808–1845) started his brief but
astonishingly fertile career. He carried to a finer development in poetry the love of nature which had informed
Christian Tullin's verse in the previous century (1728–1765),
and Wergeland also wrote voluminously and always well
in several other departments of literature. The romantic
movement, which reached Norway about 1840, had the
effect of stimulating interest in folk literature, leading to
the publication of invaluable collections of old songs, and
also to the frequent employment for literary purposes of the
Norwegian vernacular alongside the Norwego-Danish which
had previously been accepted as the standard 'literary'
language. In its further developments the romantic movement was strengthened by the establishment of a Norwegian
national drama, with Björnson (1832–1910) and Ibsen (1828–
1906) as its most notable figures. Björnson, who, like Ibsen,
had utilized legendary themes, turned afterwards to write
peasant novels. By the middle fifties, realism was swamping
romanticism, and Eilert Sundt (1817–1875) gave a strong
impetus to this change through his closely observed peasant
stories. It is common knowledge that Ibsen joined the
realistic group with his plays on modern social themes and
became its most illustrious member. For the feminist

sympathy shown in *The Doll's House* and in other plays
by Ibsen—and in some of Björnson's too—considerable
credit should be given to Camilla Collett (1813–1895),
whose novel *The Governor's Daughter* was at once a
brilliant piece of domestic naturalism and also in effect
a manifesto of the new outlook that soon revolutionized
the place and function of woman in society. The
novels of Jonas Lie (1833–1908) had a considerable
vogue in England a generation ago, and in Norwegian
literature he stands alongside Ibsen, Björnson, and others at
the head of Norway's finest period of literary production.
Lie's novels are naturalistic and analytical and cover a wide
social range. Alexander Kielland (1849–1906), a subtle and
penetrating writer whose novels and tales are unequalled in
his own country for literary beauty, pity and understanding,
is too little known abroad. Among contemporary Norwegian
novelists Knut Hamsun (*b.* 1859) and Sigrid Undset (*b.* 1882)
are outstanding—the one for a mystico-psychological type
of story *(Hunger, Pan,* and others), the other for her monumental saga in prose, *Kristin Lavransdatter.*

Before Bishop Anders Kristenson Arrebo (1587–1637),
Danish literature consisted mainly of medieval folk-songs,
and of scriptural translations by Pedersen and Bishop
Palladius which appeared between 1529 and 1550. The
early drama in Denmark followed a similar course to that
taken in other countries—namely, biblical, morality and
scholastic plays. Anders and Thomas Kingo (1634–1703)
were the true founders of poetry in the Danish vernacular,
and the latter especially did much to shape and clarify the
language for literary usage. Holberg, Tullin and Wessel
(already mentioned above) were as well known in Denmark
as in Norway, owing to the common employment of the
Norwego-Danish tongue. After the influence of Klopstock

(the great German writer, who lived in Copenhagen for some years) had diminished, Danish literature took a firm step forward in the fine lyrical poetry of Johannes Ewald (1743–1781) and the humorous satirical verse of Jens Baggesen (1764–1826), who, in their respective ways, were both poets of the first rank. Once again in the early nineteenth century, Denmark received a strong literary impulse from German sources, under (*a*) the romanticist leanings of von Staffeldt (1769–1826), who settled in Copenhagen; and (*b*) less directly through the fact that the foremost Danish poet, Ohlensschläger (1779–1850), was fired by personal contact with a Norwegian writer, Steffens, after the latter had come back from Germany imbued with romanticist ideas. The result, in Ohlensschläger's work, was a return to the past for the purpose of drawing upon the vigorous stories of northern mythology. The effect of this on the mind and spirit of Denmark was somewhat akin to that produced in Germany by the re-discovery of the *Nibelungenleid*. Christian Winther (1796–1876), a great nature poet, suffered no limitation through the regional setting of his work—in Zealand. The one Danish writer to achieve lasting world-fame is Hans Christian Andersen (1805–1875). His fairy tales and fables will continue to appeal to adults even if children should ever tire of them. Romanticism had run its course in Denmark by about the third quarter of the nineteenth century, and Jacobsen (1847–1885), Drachmann (1846–1908), and Schandorph (1836–1901) were leaders in the reaction toward realism which the well-known critic Georg Brandes (1842–1927) did much to set going, through his interest in the French realists. Carl Ewald (1856–1908), in such books as *My Little Boy*, popularized a particularly delightful kind of humanized cautionary tale.

．　　．　　．　　．　　．

In Sweden, folk-songs, biblical translations, chronicles

and romances in verse, and didactic plays held the field up
to the seventeenth century. Swedish poetry began with
Göran Lilja (1598–1672), writing as ' Georg Sternhjelm ',
but it was not until what is known as the Gustavian Period
(1771–1809) that an age of marked literary fertility came.
Two earlier eighteenth-century writers should be named :
Olaf von Dalin (1708–1763), dramatist, historian, poet, and
journalist : and Jakob Mörk (1714–1763), Sweden's first
novelist—both of whom owed much to contemporary
English writers. The mystic, Swedenborg (1688–1772),
exercised a world-wide and still active influence through a
particular channel of religious philosophy, the English poet
Blake being among those who have shown a strong mystical
kinship with Swedenborgianism. In the middle of the
Gustavian period the Swedish Academy was founded
(1786), setting up a standard of extreme conservatism in
literature which has been maintained with perhaps undue
consistency. The outstanding Gustavians, Karl Bellmann
(1740–1795) and Johan Kellgren (1751–1795) were followed
by a group of anti-academic writers known as the Phos-
phirists (1807 onward). Thence until about 1840 Swedish
poetry flourished, notably in the work of Dahlgren, Julia
Nyberg, Tegnér, and Stagnelius. Karl Almqvist (1793–
1866), a fertile and versatile man of letters, was perhaps the
most eminent author produced by Sweden during that
period and until the powerful inrush of realism brought an
entirely changed tone and atmosphere. August Strindberg
(1849–1912), after surviving a generation in which he was
attacked and derided, has won a place on the world-stage for
plays in which hatred and dementia do not disguise the
power of his turbulent genius, which, however much
embittered and self-tortured, was genius nevertheless. At
the moment, however, there are signs that extravagant
praise of Strindberg may necessitate a later moderation of
judgment. Women writers have been proportionately

numerous in Sweden, and in recent years the novels of Selma
Lagerlof (*b.* 1858) and the educational writings of Ellen
Key (*b.* 1849) are as well known abroad as in their own
country.

§ 2 —*Ibsen*

For understandable though inadequate reasons, English
interest has been too exclusively devoted to Ibsen's prose
dramas on modern themes. There were four main phases
in Ibsen's output, and it is by no means certain that the
phase we in this country have concentrated upon is the
most important. In the first place, Ibsen was a poet of high
distinction and also a great poetic dramatist —as in *Brand*
and *Peer Gynt.* Secondly, his plays on historical and
legendary themes (including *The Pretenders, Lady Inger,
Emperor and Galilean,* and *The Vikings*) sometimes touch a
majestic level. Thirdly, there are his social dramas, which
swept so strongly down a particular stream of tendency
running through Europe half a century or more ago, that
they are sometimes credited with initiating changes which,
in fact, they furthered but did not begin. Fourthly, there
is Ibsen the symbolist, who may conceivably be the pro-
foundist Ibsen of all, though his last plays hardly suggest as
much to English minds. Moreover, the incidental symbolism
introduced into some of the social dramas is occasionally
tiresome, as is the case with the little footbridge repeatedly
spoken of by Rosmer and Rebecca West in *Rosmersholm.*
If it were possible to clear the mind of all one knows about
Ibsen and his place in modern literature and thought, and
then to read his work anew from beginning to end, it is not
unlikely that *The Pretenders* might seem his greatest single
achievement. On the stage it is unforgettably impressive,
satisfying almost every canon of romantic drama, and
holding vigour, colour, and intellectual excitement in a

fair balance. Earl Skule and Bishop Nicholas are masterly character creations, while the bishop's death-scene is magnificently conducted by the author and has as much intellectual and spiritual as dramatic content. The stage action passes at Bergen and Oslo in the early thirteenth century, but, like all superlative creative achievements, *The Pretenders* escapes from the confines of time and place into the theatre of the soul. No doubt it will appear to some that to rate this play so high is a personal idiosyncrasy which does injustice to *Brand* and *Peer Gynt*. The value to be set upon these two poetic dramas must be to some extent limited, however, by the consideration that they are literary hybrids—more than poems and less than plays. *Peer Gynt* has been staged, and no experience in a theatre can quite compare with it, but it is in truth of unmanageable magnitude and its fluctuations of mood are bewildering at a single visual sitting. *Brand* is at once too massive and too bare for the stage; it lacks dramatic breadth and variety almost as completely as *Peer Gynt* has these in excess. Neither conveys quite that suggestion of imponderable genius which lifts a work beyond the necessity of observing the canons of constructive discipline, and it is not unfair to regard both as blemished masterpieces—blemished, that is, by the absence of harmony between form and substance. Yet aside from such matters, *Brand* is a superb poetic tragedy with some of the stark grandeur of Æschylus and with the Shakespearian tragic motive which makes destiny grow out of character. Brand is the great, the noble, man brought to ruin by the fatal germ within himself. His excess of goodness turns, in its practical effect, to positive evil. He exalts the abstract idea of duty and sacrifice until it becomes a fetish-altar upon which others as well as himself must be offered up. God must be given ALL—or nothing at all. He must himself give all; and as priest he must demand without a tremor of weakness or compassion that others shall give all.

The ideal having become divorced from its essential relation to reality, the ' noble ' man turns into the man possessed of a devil, reiterating his horrible cry, ' Give ! . . . Give ! . . . In the name of God, GIVE ! ' He tears his breast and the breasts of others weaker than himself with the claws of sacrifice, until at last, maimed and driven out upon the mountain-side, as the avalanche crashes down upon him he hears a Voice crying (in contradiction of the law he has given his life to proclaim), ' God is Love ! '

Whereas *Brand* might be called a Vision of Judgment, *Peer Gynt* is a Phantasmagoria of Earth. Peer plashes in the mire of half-and-half sins—is neither truly vicious nor truly virtuous ; in the end he has only the value of old metal. The Button-Moulder, the mystical figure who is to meet him again at ' the last cross-road ', tells Peer :

> [God] flings nothing away as entirely worthless
> that can be made use of as raw material.
> Now, *you* were designed as a shining button
> on the vest of the world ; but your loop gave way ;
> so into the waste-box you needs must go,
> and then, as they phrase it, be merged in the mass.[1]

Ibsen poised on this simple idea the multitudinously complex structure of *Peer Gynt*, which creates the impression that it has innumerable ' meanings ' hidden in the saeters and trolls that infest it, as well as in the boyg and the sphinx. This ' dramatic poem ' in five acts and thirty-eight scenes is a strange agglomeration of folk-drama, Christmas panto-mime, *revue*, farce, and morality play, with the exquisite character of Solveig set like a bright jewel in the midst. Its formless form gave Ibsen unlimited opportunity for the symbolistic mystification which fascinated him, and it might be quite unprofitable to pursue the faint half-meanings and vague significances that momentarily pop out their tantalizing heads and dodge them swiftly in again.

[1] Archer's translation.

A Doll's House (1879) was indubitably a landmark. It has been said that when Nora Helmer walked out of her husband's house to live her own life and banged the door behind her the sound reverberated throughout Europe. Up to that time, it seems certain, there had never been a play which startled so many people in so many widely-separated places within so short a time. It is true that the sound took more than ten years to reach English theatre audiences, though meanwhile it had shaken Norwegian society to the roots. A thoughtful young person coming upon *A Doll's House* to-day, for the first time, would probably find it far from easy to understand what all the fuss was about, both in the play and in the sensation it caused. This piece might now be renamed *What Every Woman Does* or, alternatively, *What No Woman Thinks of Doing.* What Nora did was to discover she had a soul, or a personality, or whatever we choose to call a woman's awakened ego. Nowadays, every woman either makes that discovery before she leaves the nursery, or she assumes it as a fact self-evident from the cradle and therefore never bothers to discover it at all. So far has the world moved on in fifty years. In 1879 it *was* a discovery. It nearly startled Nora out of her wits, and almost shamed Helmer into his grave. Ibsen had previously shocked Norway with *Love's Comedy*, a play in rhymed verse expressing an anti-romantic view of the preliminaries to marriage, and it was many years before the great dramatist could come out of exile with any confidence that his countrymen would receive him. When at length they did, the scene in the theatre was rapturous almost beyond description. The flood of newspaper vituperation let loose when *Ghosts* was first produced in London in the 'nineties remains unique. The serious discussion of heredi-tary disease—or indeed the introduction of any serious subject—on the stage was completely at variance with the tradition of the English drama. But before long it was the tradition that disappeared, and the new realistic drama went on. . . .

Looking back, and surveying Ibsen and Ibsenism in coolness and calm, we can now ask what were the lastingly important factors in Ibsen's plays that made him most serviceable to drama. The drama of ideas would have come without Ibsen, though he may have accelerated its coming. But the hectic and artificial form taken at first by the drama of ideas in England suggests that Ibsen's most valuable contribution to dramatic craftsmanship was his complete mastery of the naturalistic presentation of character and, through character, of ideas. It is true to say that Ibsen's characters invariably exist before the ideas ; they are born for the specific purpose of expressing the ideas, but they *are* born. Nora Helmer *is* Nora Helmer ; or, rather, Nora Helmer *is* a woman : she is not a personified Woman's Emancipation Bill nor an inert symbol of sex-equality. Though Ibsen dearly loved symbols and was inclined to leave them lying carelessly about in inappropriate places, he did not in his best years put symbols where human beings should be. All this might go without saying if it were first pointed out that his dialogue, in the realistic plays, is wholly natural. The people sit down to talk, and do talk, with the perfect ease that belongs to a *real* kitchen, or a *real* drawing-room, or a *real* study. And since the conversation is so ' natural ' (what, to be pedantic, should be said is—' since the illusion is so perfect that the conversation appears to be natural '), the characters themselves appear natural in the same degree, and the ideas given to them are fitted to them as precisely as a die to its mould.

That was Ibsen's triumph : he taught the modern stage how to talk, he gave it something worth talking about — and Bernard Shaw, with desultory assistance from others, has kept it talking ever since.

CHAPTER IX

AMERICA

§ 1—Ground Plan

FOR several generations nearly everything written about American literature dwelt lengthily upon the discussion of whether any such thing existed, or whether in fact what was called American literature was other than a province of English literature. This continued to provide material for Anglo-American controversy until round about 1914–1918. After the war, a rapidly growing English acquaintance with contemporary United States literature convinced us that transatlantic writers were producing, and profusely, books that could not possibly have been written by European authors. The cultural affiliations between America and Great Britain remained so strong up to the mid-nineteenth century that it was almost impossible for any wide divergence of ideals or intellectual outlook to appear ; and there had been no absorption of aboriginal American elements sufficient to give a native tone. Until about 1900, therefore, it was roughly accurate to say that America had produced only one writer so un-European as to make it inconceivable that he could have belonged anywhere east of the Atlantic. That one was Walt Whitman. There is still no other uniquely-American writer as great as Whitman. But at least the bonds of Europeanism have now been loosened ; and, drawing names casually from memory, there are such present-day writers as Vachel Lindsay, Theodore Dreiser, Robert Frost, and (in part) Eugene O'Neill, whose works as they stand could not have come out of Europe. This accelerated Americanization of United States literature after about three centuries of stasis, is due to the infiltration of many different types from abroad, thus upsetting the Anglo-Saxon cultural monopoly and opening up the Middle West and West to a wash of diversified influences that are merging into a new type of culture owing little allegiance to the English type. Then, too, the freeing of the slaves after the civil war in the 'sixties helped in due course to change the attitude toward negroes so fundamentally that the sentimentalism of *Uncle Tom's Cabin* has been replaced by the primitivism of *The Congo* (Vachel Lindsay) and *The Emperor Jones* (Eugene O'Neill). The change from a predominantly English New-England tradition, that held (almost unbroken except by Whitman) throughout the last century, to the polyracial and somewhat formless but virile present mood, is the most important happening in American literature since the country was first colonized.

Nothing can be said concerning the beginnings of American literature except that there are no beginnings. The travel records and historical and theological writings from about 1600 to about 1800 are not different in kind or quality from similar contemporaneous publications in England. The one outstanding name among the literary divines is that of Jonathan Edwards (1703–1758), whose works stand worthily with the classics of evangelical and conversional literature. Another relatively great book is the *Journal* of John Woolman (1720–1772) the Quaker. Among spiritual autobiographies this ranks only slightly lower than George Fox's *Journal,* and Woolman's charm has been widely appreciated since Lamb wrote in his praise. Benjamin Franklin (1706–1790), another and much greater autobiographer, is remembered chiefly on account of his activities as a publicist in support of the American Revolution and for his pioneer undertakings in electrical research. Franklin's *Autobiography* records somewhat of these matters, and also much relating to the more intimate personal life of a shrewd and in many ways delightful practical philosopher. The War of Independence (1775–1781) had its attendant political literature, with Tom Paine's pamphlets, *Common Sense* and *The Crisis* series, as noteworthy contributions. Though Paine was an Englishman, his influence was felt less in his own country than in America and France. When in the early stages the American war was going badly for the revolutionary troops, the first number of *The Crisis* literally revitalized them with its famous challenging words, ' These are the times that try men's souls.'

Washington Irving (1783–1859), America's first really eminent writer, spent many years in diplomatic service abroad, and was often charged in his lifetime with crying-up Europe to the neglect of his own country. Yet in fact he did a great service toward healing the wounds between America and England ; and if his literary sympathies were mainly attached by English eighteenth-century writers, *Rip Van Winkle* and *The Legend of Sleepy Hollow* neverthe-less brought American themes into the forefront of world literature. William Cullen Bryant (1794–1878) is more important as the forerunner of American poetry than for his own quality as a poet, though he keeps a place in anthologies. Until after 1800, the fiction written in America was almost exclusively imitative. Fenimore Cooper (1789–1851) brought out *Precaution* in 1820, but immediately felt that he was on the wrong track. He therefore determined to write a novel that ' should be purely American ', and with *The Spy* (1821) he launched the indigenous novel. Cooper, now an underrated writer, had none of the original and fiery genius that enabled Herman Melville (1819–1891) to produce in *Moby Dick* a veritable if confused masterpiece. Edgar Allen Poe (1809–1849), though more disordered than Melville, had more genuine creative force. The world knows him by his worst poems, but some of the less-known show that he was a true master of poetic magic. Poe's

Tales of Mystery and Imagination were among the first to show America's predilection for the short story, in which Poe was succeeded by many others, including Bret Harte (1839–1902) and, later, Ambrose Bierce, and O. Henry.

About 1825 America began to feel, through the westward flow of ideas, the influence of European romanticism, humanitarianism and libertarianism. As these currents flowed in they became united with a fervent religious spirit to produce 'New England transcendentalism', wherein strong emphasis was laid upon that part of man which is beyond reason and the teaching of experience—the intuitive and purely spiritual. In literature, Emerson (1803–1882) is the leading exponent of transcendentalism, though reservations would need to be made in order to distinguish certain differences between his views and the full doctrine. By some, Emerson is considered to be America's greatest writer, but he is altogether out of fashion at present and justice can hardly be done to him. His philosophy now seems little more than a vaguely airy aspiration toward spiritual uplift, expressed in a style which dilutes the apocalyptic rumblings of Carlyle with the benedictory mellifluousness of Ruskin. But to say that, is no doubt to pronounce a judgment more damaging to oneself than to the nineteenth-century prophets. Allied more or less closely in spirit with the New England group were Long-fellow (1807–1882), Whittier (1807–1892), and Lowell (1819–1891), whose nobility and rhetoric in verse the present generation is again probably competent only to misjudge. Hawthorne (1804–1864) made the New England puritan atmosphere immortally lovely in *The Scarlet Letter*; Oliver Wendell Holmes (1809–1894) added many pleasant pages to table-talk literature; and Thoreau (1817–1862), an independent genius as well as a simple-lifer, wrote one of the half-dozen best nature books in the world—*Walden, or Life in the Woods*. In Whitman (1819–1892) America found what should be her true national voice; he was a poet-prophet whose spirit and utterance were as large as the New World itself. England acknowledged the genius of Whitman before his own country did, and it is probably still true that America would prefer to regard Mark Twain (1835–1910) rather than Whitman as its representative great man. As a humorist, Twain as easily exasperates some as he delights most; but the relatively unknown Mark Twain was a greater personality than the professional funny man who caught the public ear. Perhaps he was greatest of all in *Tom Sawyer* and *Huckleberry Finn*. William Dean Howells (1837–1920) introduced realistic fiction into America, though his realism was not very real, except, possibly, in *The Rise of Silas Lapham*. He, like Henry James (1843–1916), helped once more to Europeanize American literature; but it now appears certain that that lapse has been finally repaired and an independent national literature established. Contemporary writers in the United States have vitality and enormous speculative curiosity as well as versatility, and it will be at once disappointing and astounding if the next literary renaissance does not begin somewhere between Coney Island and Hollywood.

§ 2—*Whitman*

Voltaire looked across the Atlantic and hoped the New World would produce new men. It did not. But it produced a New Man—Walt Whitman. It is idle to argue whether Whitman is or is not America's greatest writer; the point is irrelevant, however we choose to settle it. The only thing that matters about Whitman is that he was the New Man; and as such he is much more important than the New Woman, who appeared about the same time. For the New Woman has proved to be only a pathetic copy of the Old Man, whose blood had run to ink and water and his brain to dust. Whitman had fresh new blood and fresh new brains ; but the blood mattered most, for there can be no good brain without good blood. If Whitman means anything at all to us, he means it in our veins first and only afterwards in the brain. What we receive from him, if anything at all, is not a mental stimulus but a blood transfusion, which brings all other good in its train.

Yet to say that Whitman was the New Man is, after all, a misnomer. He was in truth the oldest man of all—Adam reborn :

> As Adam early in the morning,
> Walking forth from the bower refresh'd with sleep,
> Behold me where I pass, hear my voice, approach,
> Touch me. . . .[1]

Whitman did what Adam would have done if he had found himself in America instead of Eden. He went down to the sea and tuned his words to the rhythm of the waves. He looked upon the earth around him and found it stirring in him sensations and longings and aspirations that came out in oceanic force to the pattern of those sea-rhythms. And in the earth he found one phenomenon more important than any other since it was the sole key to every other— *himself*. So, in the first words of the first poem in his first book, *Leaves of Grass*, we have this :

> One's self I sing, a single separate person.

But he sang of himself not as himself alone. Though no man ever concentrated his own attention on himself with anything like Whitman's persistency and particularity, no one was ever less an egoist than Whitman. An egoist is one who draws everything inward to himself. He is a leech upon the body of the world, swelling himself disgustingly with the ichor he sucks without pause. Whitman, on the

[1] *Children of Adam.*

contrary, radiated everything outward from himself. He was a creative dynamic centre. Therefore he sang his own single separate person because through it and it alone could he ' utter the word Democratic, the word En-Masse '. We can comprehend men only in the measure that we comprehend *this man*—the Self. Socrates knew this very well and framed his chief injunction, *Know thyself*. The post-pagan doctrine of self-negation, self-mortification, selflessness, self-sacrifice, and so forth, is dangerous because it offers an easy loophole of escape from man's primary duty of knowing the one so that he may know the many. It is dreadfully easy to throw off the responsible burden of self with the claim that only so can a man be free to study and serve the mass ; but it is nevertheless sure that only as a man knows and serves the one—the self which is his special charge—only so can he know and serve the many. All else is evasion and delusion ; not holiness, but spiritual nihilism. Whitman's song was of the Whole Man, ' the Form complete ', and he found in his Self the keystone of understanding for the Whole Man. He did really sing, as he claimed,

Of Life immense in passion, pulse, and power.

For as long as a quarter of a century after his death, people were still asking ' Was Whitman a poet ? '—and replying with an impassioned negative to their own question. We cannot sensibly hold them blameworthy, for it is a reasonably sound instinct that causes men to be suspicious of newness *qua* newness. Not all new things are valid or true, and no one has yet discovered how the unfamiliar-and-true can be immediately distinguished from the unfamiliar-and-false. By 1855, when *Leaves of Grass* was published, civilized men and women had long since forgotten that, in the divine mind, they are creatures of ' passion, pulse and power '. (' Creatures of spirit ' some will say, but that, surely, was what Whitman meant by ' power '.) And having forgotten

the primal nature of their being, they found Whitman's
reminder not only new but blasphemously new—a kind of
horrible, lewd, animal, God-denying paganism :

> The earth does not argue,
> Is not pathetic, has no arrangements,
> Does not scream, haste, persuade, threaten, promise,
> Makes no discriminations, has no conceivable failures,
> Closes nothing, refuses nothing, shuts none out,
> Of all the powers, objects, states, it notifies, shuts none out.[1]

The root trouble between Whitman and his detractors was
that he remembered many things about God that they had
forgotten.   Their way of life was founded on the conviction
that ' the earth is the Lord's '.   Whitman recalled the
text's continuation : ' The earth is the Lord's *and the
fullness thereof.*'

> Such gliding wonders ! such sights and sounds !
> Such join'd unended links, each hooked to the next,
> Each answering all, each sharing the earth with all.
>
> .   .   .   .   .
>
> My spirit has passed in compassion and determination
> around the whole earth.[2]

Whitman was the first to teach the modern world the
truth about poetry and the material of poetry.   Poetry
would be a failure and a feeble fraud if its nature were in the
least degree exclusive.   But for centuries poets left a good
many things off their map—either because these were
' low ' in the intellectual sense or ' indecent ' in the sexual
sense.   Poetry must, however, be prepared to say something
about everything that comes within human experience ;
it must be the touchstone of ALL experience.   Whitman sang
of everything : of the Universe, down to the cheese-cloth
that hangs in the kitchen and the cobwebs festooning from
the rafters.   As to subjects that are ' improper ', he believed
with all his force (though he did not say with this brevity)

---

[1] *A Song of the Rolling Road.*   [2] *Salut au Monde.*

that nothing is indecent but the sense of indecency. Those who suffer under the affliction of this sense find it virtually impossible to look beyond their sex-obsession (or anti-sex obsession—the two are identical) ; so that they never truly discover Whitman, whose only offence was that he could find nothing indecent in God's creation, and he gladly filled his capacious heart with the limitless provision afforded in that creation. The puritan's dilemma is first that he finds it impossible to believe in the existence of purity on earth ; and secondly that he altogether misunderstands the nature of purity—regarding it as emasculate and ascetic instead of robustly healthy and joyous and overflowing with the gladness-of-being-alive. Expecting purity to walk demurely with folded hands, when he finds it singing with delight and leaping in ecstasy he denies that it is purity, calls it pagan lust and is sure it will come to a bad end. Whitman gladly accepted sex as a potent factor in human experience just as he gladly accepted the sun ; and he placed it high among man's activities because it is the procreant fountain of life :

> Sex contains all, bodies, souls,
> Meanings, proofs, purities, delicacies, results, promulgations,
> Songs, commands, health, pride, the maternal mystery,
>   the seminal milk,
> All hopes, benefactions, bestowals, all the passions, loves,
>   beauties, delights of the earth. . . .[1]

Whitman stood for the active and positive life ; he hated whatever was impassive and null :

> Now I will dismiss myself from impassive women,
> I will go stay with her who waits for me, and with those women
>   who are full-blooded and sufficient for me.[2]

If Whitman's work is read in full it will be found that sex is far from being disproportionately stressed—it is one theme among many, one element in the full life of the

---

[1] *A Woman waits for Me* (*Children of Adam*).   [2] Ibid.

whole man. He might without unbalance have given it a
larger place, for although the world will not be saved by
sex alone, it cannot be saved at all until the basic sexual
maladjustments inherent in our present civilization are
rectified.

The other chief charges preventing an early acknowledg-
ment of Whitman's genius were (a) that the general content
of his poetry was unpoetical, and (b) that his verse was
neither metrical nor musical. There is no need to dwell
upon (a), in view of the claim made above that there are
no ' poetic subjects ' with which alone poetry may deal.
But about Whitman's free verse something needs to be
said. The view that he is not musical can best be tested
by asking whether the sound of running water is musical,
or the wash of the tides, or the wind in the trees. It would
be useless to attempt to justify Whitman to those who
answer ' No '. And to those who answer ' Yes ; those *are*
musical ', there is little need to do more than suggest that
Whitman's music is of that kind. Generations had been
brought up to believe that a strongly defined metre and a
recognizable recurrent pattern were necessary to both
music and poetry. These factors may or may not be
desirable ; they certainly are not essential—except for
readers who like their poetry to resemble cheap wall-paper.
Inasmuch as Whitman's verse is made in the audible likeness of natural forces and not according to the then-familiar
literary practice, its movement is rhythmical, not metrical.
Metre is no more than the babyhood of rhythm ; a five-
finger exercise compared with a Beethoven symphony.
Metres are devised according to a pattern small enough to
be *perceptibly* recurrent. The pattern of rhythm may be
so extensive as to be imperceptible in its completeness.
There is a pattern that *can be seen* in the surface movement
of a pool when a stone is dropped into the water : it is a
recurrent (metrical) pattern with a narrow range of regular

intervals. There is a pattern also, but too extensive to be perceived by any physical faculty, in the movement of the tides of all the oceans : the recurrent (rhythmical) pattern is too enormous for sight or hearing to encompass its whole. The difference between metre and rhythm, then, is a difference of magnitude and of counterchange and variety. It might be expressed arithmetically as the difference between, say, $\cdot\dot{9}$ and $\cdot18325094 6\dot{7}$. Expressed in terms of verse it is the difference between

> ' Ba, ba, black sheep, have you any wool ? '
> ' Yes sir, yes sir, three bags full '

and

> In cabin'd ships at sea,
> The boundless blue on every side expanding,
> With whistling wind and music of the waves, the large
>   imperious waves,
> Or some lone bark buoy'd on the dense marine,
> Where joyous, full of faith, spreading white sails,
> She cleaves the ether mid the sparkle and the foam of day,
>   or under many a star at night,
> By sailors young and old haply will I, a reminiscence of the
>   land, be read,
> In full rapport at last.[1]

Even traditional poets, whose technical models are literary more than natural, tend according to the measure of their greatness to move away from metre to the larger control of rhythm, as we may see in Shakespeare and Milton—especially in *Samson Agonistes*, where the terrific force of spiritual energy cuts its own channel of utterance and fuses Miltonic blank verse in the crucible of *vers libre*.

---

[1] Whitman : *In Cabin'd Ships at Sea* (*Inscriptions*).

TIME CHARTS

These comparative tables have been simplified to the utmost degree and include only a selection of those writers whose works have a more than national reputation. The authors have been grouped according to the periods in which they flourished, not necessarily according to dates of birth.   To be really graphic the charts should be drawn to scale, in order to show an accurate time-relation ; but if prepared to a scale of only one inch to a year, a total length of more than 72 yards would be required to cover the period from 700 B.C. to A.D. 1900.

	GREECE	ROME
Before 700 B.C.	Homer	—
	Hesiod	—
↑ 500	Æschylus	—
	Sophocles	—
	Euripides	—
	Herodotus	—
	Thucydides	—
	Aristophanes	—
400	Socrates	—
	Xenophon	—
	Plato	—
	Demosthenes	—
	Aristotle	—
300	Theocritus	—
	—	Plautus
200		
	—	Terence
100 B.C.	—	Cicero
	—	Caesar
	—	Lucretius
	—	Catullus
	—	Vergil
	—	Horace
	—	Livy
A.D.	—	Ovid
	—	Seneca
100 A.D.	Plutarch	—
↓		Marcus Aurelius
200	—	

A.D.	ENGLAND	FRANCE
circa 600	*Beowulf*	—
↑	Caedmon. Cynewulf	—
900	Bede. King Alfred	—
	—	*Chanson de Roland*
	—	Troubadours
1200	Early religious plays	—
	Ballads	*Roman de la Rose*
1300		
	Wyclif. Gower	—
	Langland. Chaucer	—
1400		
	Scottish vernacular poets	Villon
1500	More. Tyndale	—
	Wyat. Surrey	Rabelais
	Spenser. Bacon	Ronsard
	Marlowe. Shakespeare	Montaigne
1600	Ben Jonson	—
	Authorized Version of Bible	Corneille. Molière
	Sir Thomas Browne	Racine. Pascal
	Milton	La Fontaine
	Bunyan	—
	Dryden	—
	Wycherley	—
	Congreve	—
↓		
1700		

GERMANY	ITALY	OTHER COUNTRIES
—	—	—
—	—	—
National Epics : *Hildebrandslied,* *Nibelungenlied,* etc.	— — —	— — Scandinavian Sagas
— —	— Dante	— —
— —	Petrarch Boccaccio	— —
—	—	SPAIN: *Amadis de Gaula*
Luther — — *Faust-book*	— Machiavelli Ariosto Tasso	— — — SPAIN : Cervantes Lope de Vega
— — — — — — — —	— — — — — — — —	— — SPAIN : Calderon — — — — —

	ENGLAND	FRANCE
1700 ↑	Defoe. Swift	—
	Addison. Steele	Voltaire
	Pope	—
	Richardson. Fielding	*Encyclopedists :*
	Johnson. Burke	Diderot, etc.
	Sterne. Smollett	—
	—	Rousseau
	Goldsmith. Sheridan	—
	Burns. Blake	—
1800	Wordsworth. Coleridge	—
	Scott. Byron	Stendhal
	Jane Austen	Balzac
	Shelley. Keats	Victor Hugo
	Lamb. Hazlitt	Dumas
	Dickens. Thackeray	George Sand
	Brontës. George Eliot	Baudelaire
	Tennyson. Browning	Flaubert
	Carlyle. Ruskin	Zola
	Swinburne. Rossetti	Verlaine
	Meredith. Hardy	Maupassant
1900	Stevenson. Wilde	Anatole France

GERMANY	ITALY	OTHER COUNTRIES
—	—	—
—	Goldoni	NORWAY : Holberg
Klopstock	—	SWEDEN : Swedenborg
Lessing	—	—
—	—	—
—	—	—
Goethe	Alfieri	—
Schiller	—	—
—	—	—
—	—	RUSSIA : Pushkin, Gogol,
—	Manzoni	Turgenev, Dostoevsky,
Heine	—	Tolstoy, Chekhov
—	Leopardi	—
—	—	AMERICA : Emerson,
—	Mazzini	Poe, Hawthorne, Long-
—	—	fellow, Whitman
—	Carducci	
Wagner	—	NORWAY : Ibsen,
—	—	Björnson
Karl Marx	—	—
—	—	SWEDEN : Strindberg

READING LIST

PRINCIPAL WORKS IN ENGLISH TRANSLATION [1]

*' Woe to the translator who gives a literal version—enervating the sense
and extinguishing the fire. In this connection one may justly affirm that
the letter kills but the spirit quickens.'*—VOLTAIRE

I.—GREECE

HOMER (before 700 B.C.)

Iliad : Trans. in verse, G. Chapman (*Chatto*) ; A. Pope
(*various editions*).
Trans. in prose, Lang, Leaf, and Myers (*Macmillan*)
Story of the Iliad (prose trans.), Marvin, Mayor, and
Stawell (*Dent*)

Odyssey : Trans. in verse, G. Chapman (*Chatto*)
Trans. in prose, Butcher and Lang (*Macmillan*)
Story of the Odyssey (prose trans.), Marvin, Mayor,
and Stawell (*Dent.*)

HESIOD (before 700 B.C.)

Poems and Fragments : Trans. in prose, A. W. Mair (*Oxford
Press*)

ÆSCHYLUS (525–456 B.C.)

Plays : Trans. J. S. Blackie (*Everyman*)
Plays : Trans. Lewis Campbell (*World's Classics*)
Oresteia : Trans. Gilbert Murray (*Allen & Unwin*)

SOPHOCLES (495–405 B.C.)

Plays : Trans. Sir George Young (*Everyman*)
Plays : Trans. Lewis Campbell (*World's Classics*)

[1] ' *Everyman* ', following a title, indicates that the translation is
included in the Everyman's Library published by J. M. Dent & Sons,
Ltd. The World's Classics are issued by the Oxford University Press.

EURIPIDES (480–406 B.C.)
> Plays : Trans. Gilbert Murray (*Allen & Unwin*)

ARISTOPHANES (448–385 B.C.)
> Plays : Trans. J. P. Maine (*Everyman*)
> Plays : Trans. Hookham Frere (*World's Classics*)

HERODOTUS (*c.* 484–428 B.C.)
> History : Trans. Rawlinson (*Everyman*)

THUCYDIDES (*c.* 471–400 B.C.)
> Peloponnesian War : Trans. Crawley (*Everyman*)

XENOPHON (*c.* 430–350 B.C.)
> Cyropaedia : Trans. revised by F. M. Stawell (*Everyman*)

PLATO (427–347 B.C.)
> Republic : Trans. Jowett (*Oxford Press*)
> Trans. Spens (*Everyman*)

DEMOSTHENES (384–322 B.C.)
> On the Crown and other Orations : Trans. C. Rann Kennedy
> (*Everyman*)

ARISTOTLE (384–322 B.C.)
> Ethics : Trans. D. P. Chase (*Everyman*)
> Politics : Trans. Jowett (*Oxford Press*)

THEOCRITUS (*fl.* 283–263 B.C.)
> Idylls : Trans. Calverley (*Bell*)

II.—ROME

PLAUTUS, Titus Maccius (*c.* 250–184 B.C.)
> Comedies : Trans. H. T. Riley (*Bell*)
> Three Plays : Trans. F. A. Wright and H. L. Rogers
> (*Routledge*)

CICERO, Marcus Tullius (106–43 B.C.)
> Essays and Letters : Various translators (*Everyman*)

CAESAR, Gaius Julius (102-44 B.C.)
> Gallic War, etc. : Trans. W. A. McDevitte (*Everyman*)

LUCRETIUS [Titus Lucretius Carus] (*c.* 98–55 B.C.)
 On the Nature of Things : Trans. W. E. Leonard (*Everyman*)

VERGIL [Publius Vergilius Maro] (70–19 B.C.)
 Æneid, Georgics, Eclogues : Trans. Dryden (*World's Classics*) ;
  trans. J. Rhoades (*World's Classics*)
 Æneid : Trans. E. Fairfax-Taylor (*Everyman*)

HORACE [Quintus Horatius Flaccus] (65–8 B.C.)
 Complete Poems : Various translators (*Everyman*)

LIVY [Titus Livius] (59 B.C.–A.D. 19)
 History of Rome : Trans. Canon Roberts (*Everyman*)

SENECA, Lucius Annæus (5 B.C.–A.D. 65)
 Tragedies : Trans. in verse E. I. Harris (*Oxford Press*)

MARCUS AURELIUS ANTONINUS (A.D. 121–80)
 Meditations : Trans. John Jackson (*World's Classics*)

III.—FRANCE

RABELAIS, François (*c.* 1500–53)
 Gargantua and Pantagruel : Trans. Urquhart (*Everyman*)

MONTAIGNE, Michel Eyquem de (1533–92)
 Essays : Trans. Florio (*World's Classics* and *Everyman*)

MOLIÈRE [Jean Baptiste Poquelin] (1622–73)
 Plays : Various translators (*Everyman*)

RACINE, Jean (1639–99)
 Esther ; Britannicus ; Iphigenia : Trans. R. B. Boswell (*Bell*)

PASCAL, Blaise (1623–62)
 Pensées : Trans. W. F. Trotter (*Everyman*)

LA FONTAINE, Jean de (1621–95)
 Fables : Trans. E. Marsh (*Heinemann*)

VOLTAIRE [François Arouet] (1694–1778)
 Letters from England (*Peter Davies*)
 Age of Louis XIV : Trans. M. P. Pollack (*Everyman*)
 Candide

Rousseau, Jean Jacques (1712–78)
  Emile : Trans. B. Foxley (*Everyman*)
  The Social Contract (*Everyman*)
  Confessions (*Everyman*)

Stendhal [Henri Beyle] (1783–1842)
  The Charterhouse of Parma : Trans. Scott Moncrieff (*Chatto*)

Balzac, Honoré de (1799–1850)
  Chief novels : Various translators (*Everyman* and *Collins'*
    Illustrated Classics)

Hugo, Victor (1802–85)
  Chief novels (*Everyman*)

Dumas, Alexandre (1803–70)
  Chief novels (*Everyman*)

George Sand [Mme Dudevant, *née* Dupin] (1804–76)
  The Devil's Pool, etc. (*Everyman*)

Flaubert, Gustave (1821–80)
  Salammbo : Trans. J. S. Chartres (*Everyman*)
  Madame Bovary : Trans. E. Marx-Aveling (*Everyman*)

Maupassant, Guy de (1850–93)
  Complete novels and stories : Various translators (*Knopf*)

Anatole France [Jacques Anatole François Thibault] (1844–1924)
  Works : Various translators (*John Lane*)

IV.—ITALY

Dante Alighieri (1265–1321)
  The Divine Comedy : Trans. Cary (*Everyman*)

Petrarch [Francesco Petrarca] (1304–74)
  Love Songs : Trans. W. D. Foulke (*Oxford Press*)

Boccaccio, Giovanni (1313–75)
  Decameron : Trans. J. M. Rigg (*Everyman*)

MACHIAVELLI, Niccolo (1469–1527)

    The Prince : Trans. Luigi Ricci (*World's Classics*)
    History of Florence (*Everyman*)

MANZONI, Allessandro (1785–1873)

    The Betrothed : Unnamed translator (*Bell*)

LEOPARDI, Giacomo (1798–1837)

    Poems : Trans. G. L. Bickersteth (*Cambridge Press*)

MAZZINI, Giuseppe (1805–72)

    Duties of Man, etc. (*Everyman*)

V.—SPAIN

CERVANTES [Miguel de Cervantes Saavedra] (1547–1616)

    Don Quixote : Trans. Motteux (*Everyman*)

CALDERON [Pedro Calderon de la Barca] (1600–81)

    Six Plays : Trans. FitzGerald (*Everyman*)

VI.—GERMANY

THE NIBELUNGENLIED :

    Trans. Margaret Armour (*Everyman*)

LESSING, Gotthold Ephraim (1729–81)

    Laocoön : Minna von Barnhelm ; Nathan the Wise (*Everyman*)

GOETHE, Johan Wolfgang (1749–1832)

    Faust : Trans. A. G. Latham (*Everyman*)
    Wilhelm Meister : Trans. Carlyle (*Everyman*)

SCHILLER, Johann (1759–1805)

    Works : Various translators (*Bell*)

HEINE, Heinrich (1799–1856)

    Book of Songs : Trans. J. Todhunter (*Oxford Press*)

WAGNER, Richard (1813–83)

    The Ring of the Nibelung : Trans. in verse Randle Fynes
    (*Heinemann*)

Marx, Karl (1818–83)
    Capital : Trans. E. and C. Paul (*Everyman*)

Nietzsche, Friedrich (1844–1900)
    Thus Spake Zarathustra : Trans. T. Common (*Allen & Unwin*)
    Beyond Good and Evil : Trans. T. Common (*Allen & Unwin*)

VII.—RUSSIA

Pushkin, Alexander (1799–1837)
    Boris Godunov : Trans. A. Hayes (*Routledge*)

Gogol, Nicholas (1809–52)
    Dead Souls : Trans. C. J. Hogarth (*Everyman*)

Turgenev, Ivan (1818–83)
    Chief novels : Trans. Constance Garnett (*Heinemann*)

Dostoevsky, Feodor (1821–81)
    Chief novels : Trans. Constance Garnett (*Heinemann*)

Tolstoy, Leo (1828–1910)
    Works : Trans. Louise and Aylmer Maude (*World's Classics*)

Chekhov, Anton (1860–1904)
    Plays and Stories : Trans. Constance Garnett (*Chatto*)

VIII.—SCANDINAVIA

Ibsen, Henrik (1828–1906)
    Plays, etc. : Trans. by W. Archer and others (*Heinemann*)
    Brand : Trans. F. E. Garrett (*Everyman*)
    Peer Gynt : Trans. R. Farquharson Sharp (*Everyman*)
    Plays : Trans. R. Farquharson Sharp (*Everyman*)

Björnson, Björnstjerne (1832–1910)
    Plays : Trans. R. Farquharson Sharp (*Everyman*)

Strindberg, August (1849–1912)
    Plays : Various translators (*Cape*)

INDEX